WESTWOOD 2000

Above: Tower of St. Mary the Virgin, Westwood (S. Snailum)

Cover: The entrance to the quarry, 1895
© Crown Copyright/MOD

Overleaf: Ordnance Survey map of 1901.

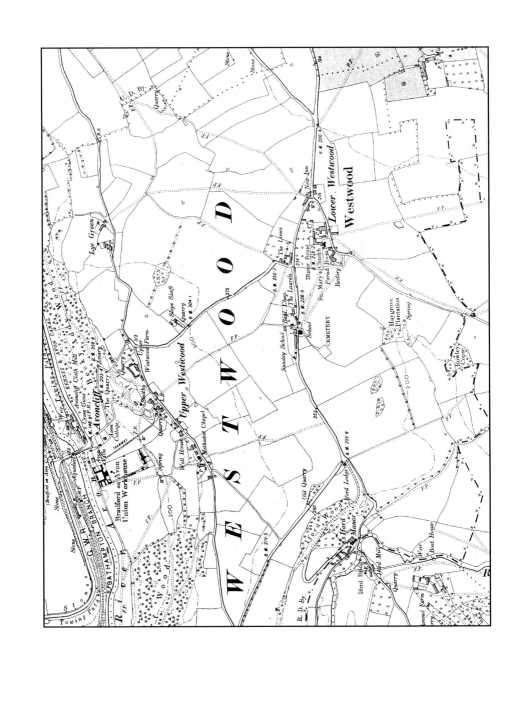

WESTWOOD
~ 2000 ~

Reflections on a Village

Compiled by Susan Snailum

ELSP

Published in 2000 by
ELSP
1 The Shambles
Bradford on Avon
Wiltshire   BA15 1JS

in association with
Westwood Millennium Project

Design and typesetting by
Ex Libris Press
1 The Shambles
Bradford on Avon
Wiltshire

Printed by
Cromwell Press
Trowbridge
Wiltshire

ISBN 1 093341 57 4

CONTENTS

INTRODUCTION & ACKNOWLEDGEMENTS

At the turn of the century many people were thinking about the next Millennium and what it may bring. But before stepping over the threshold to the future, it was important to look back and see what had been achieved. At that point, villages throughout the land began to think of putting together a book telling the story so far. And I thought, why should Westwood be any different - why not have a book about Westwood up to the year 2000. I proposed the idea to David Stockwell and Terry Biles and, between us, we got the project off the ground, with support from the Parish Council, and help and encouragement from Mike Marshman, Local Studies and Reference Librarian at Trowbridge Reference Library.

This is not, nor does it pretend to be, the definitive, learned tome about Westwood. There are sections which have been contributed by experts in their field and these are interspersed with snippets of local interest and many village voices recalling past events. A copy of the book will be lodged in the Wiltshire County Archive for future historians; meanwhile, I hope that it will prove of interest to the present generation.

I would like to acknowledge with gratitude the help and support I received from so many.

When the idea was first launched a band of helpers distributed the "census" forms to every house in the village - and then collected them. Terry and Sheila Biles have analysed the information in them and Sue Wood has analysed, for comparison, the 1881 census. Pat Hobbs and David Windo produced, between them, a wonderful collection of old photographs: Derek Parker has made copies of these and the negatives will be held in the County Archive. Thanks also to Ros Bartlett for being the liaison between Westwood and the Records Office in Trowbridge and for sorting the maps; and to Fiona Sultana for putting it all together for Roger Jones of Ex Libris Press. The section on Avoncliff has been produced by Paul Melling, Freda Ferne and Richard Read.

There are too many to thank individually but I am grateful to all who helped in whatever way and to those who were willing to talk to me of their recollections.

Susan Snailum

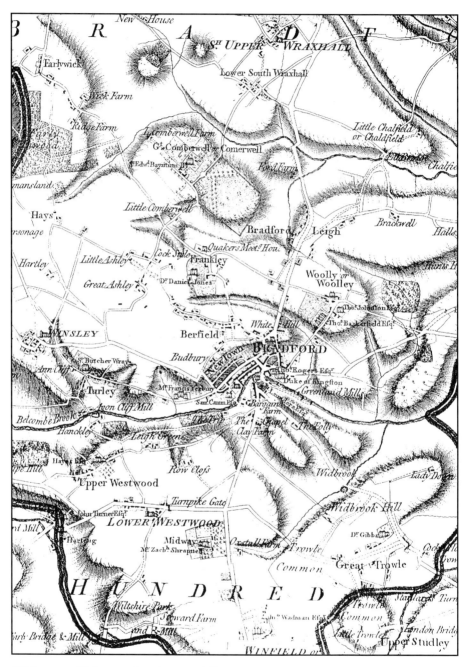

1773 map of Westwood and Avoncliff

8

The Making of Westwood

A PLAQUE ON the gateway to the parish church celebrates the fact that Westwood was recorded as a community in William the Conqueror's great Domesday Book of AD 1086. Nearly a thousand years of recorded history is something well worth celebrating.

Westwood's history can be traced back for a hundred years before 1086, but beyond that point the written records tell us nothing at all about our village. We have to rely on what can be found in the soil. This essay looks both forwards and backwards from 1086, using what few pieces of evidence we can find to chart how a few scattered farms gradually became today's Westwood.

The Remote Past

Ten thousand years ago, much of Wiltshire was still covered in the dense forest which had grown up after the last ice age. Early hunters roamed the land, following long-accustomed routes through the forest but never staying for long in any one place. One such group passed through what is now Westwood, and stopped to sharpen their flint-tipped spears and arrows. Perhaps they camped overnight. We will never know. The flints survive, but any traces left in the soil by an overnight campsite have long since faded and vanished.

Five thousand years ago, however, the first farmers began to clear patches of forest for fields and to establish permanent settlements. One such settlement was in Lower Westwood.

The low hill where the church and rectory now stand must have been a good place for a farming settlement. It was close to the spring-line where water seeped out from under the limestone, and overlooked the light soils on the flatter land towards Trowbridge. On this low hill, some time around 3000 BC, at least one Neolithic family seems to have made its home.

The evidence for this is a small piece of greenish stone, found nearby. It is part of a polished stone axe-head, once fitted to a wooden handle. It may have been part of a village carpenter's tool-bag, since it is quite small and more suited for shaping wood for rafters, ploughs and furniture rather than for felling trees and clearing woodland.

The green stone of which the axe-head was made shows that it was brought from Cornwall. For most purposes at that time, axe-heads made of flint from Salisbury Plain would have been adequate. However, good quality work required sharp-edged tools made from hard volcanic stone of the sort found along the western shores of Britain.

The axe-head may have arrived by way of trade and barter, or it may have come as a gift. At that time, inter-community trading agreements, border treaties and even dynastic marriages seem to have been sealed by the formal exchange of valuable gifts and many Cornish-made items have been found in Wiltshire.

For the moment, that is all we have. We cannot go digging up the churchyard or the rectory garden looking for prehistoric Westwood. By looking at properly excavated examples elsewhere, however, we can guess that the Westwood settlement might have been home to an extended family of about fifty people - parents, grandparents, uncles, aunts and cousins. They would have lived in wooden houses smeared with clay and thatched with reeds or straw. Although the Lower Westwood folk were almost certainly farmers, there may also have been small settlements of fishermen near Avoncliff or down by the River Frome at Iford.

At the time when the little green stone axe-head was being used at Westwood, similar axes were being used to shape the timbers for great timber circles at Avebury, Stonehenge and Stanton Drew. These three temples were later marked by enormous slabs of stone, but many other smaller timber circles were left unmarked. Every settlement seems to have had access to one and the Westwood farmers probably had a timber circle somewhere nearby.

The next two thousand years are a blank as far as Westwood is concerned. The descendants of the early farmers probably continued to farm the land, but as yet we have no trace of them. By around 500 BC, however, the population on the hills on both sides of the River Avon had increased to the point where all the available economic resources were being exploited. Competition for land led to open warfare and great hill-forts crowned the hills around Bath. The nearest one to Westwood was at Budbury, but that was two miles away on the other side of the Avon and the Westwood folk may have owed allegiance to a chief who lived in a hill fort on the same side of the river, south of Bath.

Roman Westwood

The arrival of the Roman legions probably had little immediate effect on the Westwood farmers. Apart from the replacement of the Celtic tribal aristocracy by imperial officials, things probably went on much as before. Eventually, however, the creation of the elegant spa town of Aquae Sulis around the old sacred springs at Bath led to the building of big villas all around the outskirts of the town.

These country houses depended on the new town to market their produce and to provide the luxury imports that made life in a far-flung province of the Empire worth living. Their estates had to be organised so as to yield the maximum in the way of grain, leather and wool. There are two sites in Westwood where Roman pottery has been found: one near the parish church, the other on the sloping ground to east of Housel's Field. Neither of them is likely to have been a villa. They are more likely to have been small tenant-farms on the estate of a large villa somewhere nearer Bath. On one of them, more than a century ago, a small child was found buried in a stone coffin - our first known Westwood resident.

Many of the small square fields which had been laid out during the previous thousand years still remained in use. Traces of them can be seen from the air on the lighter soils towards Trowbridge. However, a rising population led to a demand for increased production on the villa estates. This in turn led to the felling of what remained of the old forests on the heavier soils to create new farmland. The two Westwood tenant farmers would have had to contend with a harsh land agent representing the interests of the rich villa owner down the road.

Into a Dark Age

Eventually, the Roman Empire collapsed in on itself. A series of plagues had resulted in a catastrophic drop in population, and many villa estates turned from arable farming to stock-farming, which was less labour-intensive. Street-crime on the Roman roads undermined commercial confidence and the circulation of mass-produced luxury goods gradually ceased. Although Bath continued to provide a local market, it was no longer the place it had been.

In the countryside, the villa owners reorganised their estates so as to produce the everyday items they had once been able to buy in the market towns. Many of them foreclosed their tenancies, replacing tenant families with villa-based work gangs. The two Westwood farms may have suffered a similar fate.

The collapse of the Imperial administration meant that the local British aristocracy reasserted itself. Native kingdoms sprang up, based on places like Bath and Cirencester. Townsfolk and villa owners strove to maintain the old Roman way of life as their world fell about them.

Into this vacuum came the Saxons, pushing up from Hampshire. For a while, the British kingdoms held out. Around AD 500, a crucial battle on a hill near Bath stemmed the onslaught for the next fifty years: we don't know the name of the British commander, though later generations said he was called Arthur!

By AD 652, it was all over. In that year, King Cenwalh of the West Saxons fought a battle at Bradenford be Afne - the "broad ford across the Avon". From then on, Bradford was a Saxon royal estate, and Westwood (as its name suggests) was its western wood.

Bradford's Western Wood

In the centuries following the collapse of Roman rule, the woodlands expanded - in many cases covering the abandoned fields of the old villa estates. Wiltshire was now almost as tree-covered as it had been at the start of the Roman period, and Westwood was probably no longer an open landscape of small fields and hedges. Wild animals had become more frequent in the woodland and the human population had probably slumped to what it was before the Romans came.

The new Saxon royal estates depended on a good mix of arable, pasture and woodland, with different parts of the estate providing different materials. Bradford's "western wood" probably provided timber for building, charcoal for fuel and acorns for pigs. It may also have been a hunting ground for the king's sport.

The woodcutters, charcoal-burners and swineherds of this western wood were probably still British, rather than Saxon: indeed, they were probably the descendants of the people who had farmed the land here before the Romans came. All that had happened was that Saxon royal officials had replaced the Roman villa-owner's land agent.

Some time in the 10th century, Bradford's western wood came to be regarded as a separate entity – a resource that could be used by royalty to reward warriors or loyal officials. In AD 983, King Aethelraed II (later known as "the unready") gave the wood to a man called Alfnoth. A few years later he re-awarded the wood to his huntsman, Leofwine – perhaps so that he could maximise its value to the king for hunting, should he ever come to Bradford.

Alfnoth and Leofwine are the first names we can associate with Westwood. It's not clear whether these men ever lived here. Later, Westwood was to have a long history of absentee landlords, and the pattern may have been set now, with affairs managed by a local official or reeve, acting on the landlord's behalf.

The overall landlord remained the King Aethelraed. Westwood does not seem to have been part of the land in and around Bradford which the king gave to Shaftesbury Abbey in AD 1001. Instead, it seems to have been amongst the estates given by him to his queen, Emma, as part of her dowry.

After Aethelraed's death, Emma re-married. Her new husband was Cnut of Denmark, the Viking who had driven Aethelraed off the throne of England and made himself king. Emma must have been a remarkable woman. The daughter of the Duke of Normandy, she managed to outlive both Aethelraed and Cnut. In AD 1043 she gave her estate at Westwood as an endowment for the monks of St Swithun's cathedral at Winchester, in memory of her second husband. So began the long connection of Westwood with Winchester, which was to continue for almost nine hundred years.

The Domesday Survey

The Norman Conquest of England, begun in AD 1066, brought no immediate changes to Westwood. There may have been a new reeve, representing the new Norman administration of the cathedral in Winchester, but for most people life probably went on much as before.

In AD 1085, there was an invasion scare – yet more Vikings from Denmark! In the event, the attack never came, but King William determined to be well prepared for any future occasion. To resist an attack on his realm, he needed to know the wealth of each of his barons, so that he could demand from them an appropriate number of knights to assist with national defence.

To gather this information, William appointed commissioners to go from county to county across the length and breadth of England, visiting every estate to find out what it was worth. Evidence was taken from the royal shire-reeves, the local manor-reeves and from six men from each village. The information was written down in what we now know as "the Domesday Book".

The entry for Westwode gives us our first glimpse of our village as a working community. The estate was said to cover about 350 acres: however, this was an old assessment for taxation, and the true extent may well have been just over 400 acres. The estate was not being well-managed, for although the Domesday commissioners considered that there was enough arable land to need five plough-teams, there were only four teams working at the time of their visit and the yearly value of the estate had dropped from £6 to just £4.

Two-thirds of the estate was demesne land. This was the home-farm belonging to the monks at Winchester, all the produce of which went to feed the monks. Three of the four plough-teams worked on the demesne, where there were three slaves. The remaining part of the estate was farmed by ten families, who had to share the same plough-team: they also had to work for one or two days each week on the monks' demesne farm, supplementing the work of the three slaves. Life was far from easy for these families.

The arable land probably still consisted of small square fields carved out of the woodland, much as it had done in the Roman period. There were six acres of hay-meadow. No grazing land is mentioned, which is odd since the oxen which pulled the four ploughs must have grazed somewhere. Another oddity is the small amount of woodland – just 20 acres, which isn't a lot for somewhere still called "the western wood". Perhaps there was more woodland in the untaxed part of the estate.

There was also a water-driven corn mill, an important item on an estate like Westwood. The mill was probably at Avoncliff, although the first specific mention of a mill there doesn't occur until much later.

With only thirteen peasant families, plus the families of the miller and the manor-reeve, the population of Westwood can hardly have been more than a hundred. One family presumably lived in the mill at Avoncliff. Another two or three families may have lived at Iford, where there was a small hamlet which was part of the Westwood estate.

The other families probably lived in what is now Lower Westwood. There are no accurate maps of the village in the Middle Ages, but a map of 1792 shows a small enclosed area there with the main road running through it. Since the church and churchyard seem to have been added to the south side of this area in the early 13th century, it may preserve the outline of the Domesday village where the other peasant families lived, together with the manor-reeve and the three demesne slaves.

Their houses would probably have been built of timber, the spaces between the main frames being filled with panels of woven hazel smeared with clay. At this date, stone was still an expensive commodity and men who knew how to make mortar were not to be found in every village. Wood and clay, on the other hand, were cheap and everyone knew how to use them.

At the time of the Domesday survey there was probably no church in Westwood. The estate was part of Bradford parish, and originally Westwood folk would probably have had to walk to Bradford to worship, marry, and christen their children or to bury their dead. Nor would there have been a manor house, since the lord of the manor was the Prior of St Swithun's cathedral, far away in Winchester.

The Growth of the Community

For the Prior of St Swithun's, Westwood was a small distant estate. He is very unlikely ever to have come here. The manor-reeve would have had to go to Winchester once a year to present his accounts, and a cathedral official may have come to Westwood once in a while to see that all was well. Otherwise there can have been little direct contact.

The civil war between King Stephen and the Empress Mathilda, which racked England from 1139 until 1150, may not have affected Westwood much, although the king laid siege to Humphrey de Bohun's castle in nearby Trowbridge. The royal troops took the opportunity to lay waste much of the farmland round about the town. Perhaps Westwood, being part of the Winchester cathedral estates, was left alone – the Bishop of Winchester was, after all, the king's brother!

It was not until the beginning of the 13th century that the cathedral made any real investment on its estate at Westwood. Parts of the parish church may date from about this time: presumably the population had increased and it was now worth building them a chapel in the village. It may have been quite small, possibly no bigger than the chancel of the present church.

William holds 2 hides of this land from the Bishop; the previous holder could not withdraw from the church. Value of this manor when the Bishop acquired it, £6; value now of the lordship, £9; of what William holds, £3.

6 WESTWOOD. Before 1066 it paid tax for 3 hides. Land for 5 ploughs. Of this land 2 hides in lordship; 3 ploughs there; 3 slaves.
6 villagers and 4 smallholders with 1 plough.
A mill which pays 10s; meadow, 6 acres; woodland 2 furlongs long and 1 furlong wide.
Value when the Bishop acquired it, £6; now £4.

7 WROUGHTON. Before 1066 it paid tax for 30 hides. Land for 12 ploughs. Of this land 15 hides in lordship; 4 ploughs there; 3 slaves.
25 villagers and 14 smallholders have 7 ploughs.
6 mills which pay 42s 6d; meadow, 60 acres; pasture ½ league long and 3 furlongs wide; woodland, 20 acres.
A man-at-arms has 1½ hides of this land; he has 1 plough. Godric, who held it before 1066, could not be separated from the church.
Value when the Bishop acquired it, £14; value now, £18.

8 The Bishop holds BUSHTON himself. Before 1066 it paid tax for 10 hides. Land for 5 ploughs. Of this land 6½ hides in lordship; 2 ploughs there; 3 slaves.
7 villagers and 3 Cottagers with 2 ploughs.
Meadow, 30 acres; woodland 2 furlongs long and 1 furlong wide.
Value when the Bishop acquired it, £3; now £6.

9 The Bishop also holds
WANBOROUGH. Before 1066 it paid tax for 19 hides. Land for 10 ploughs. Of this land 9 hides in lordship; 3 ploughs there; 6 slaves.
19 villagers and 13 smallholders with 5 ploughs.
A mill which pays 5s; meadow, 40 acres; pasture ½ league long and 15 furlongs wide. Richere holds 1 hide of this land.
Value when the Bishop acquired it, £15; now £18.

De ead tra ten Witts.II.hid de epo. Qui ante eu
tenuit.ñ poterat ab æccta recedere.
Valuit hoc Ɔ.VI.lib q̃do eps recep.Modo dñium
ual.IX.lib. Qd Witts ten.III.lib.

Idem eps ten WESTWODE. T.R.E.geldb p.III.hid.
Tra.V.car.De hac tra.II.hidæ in dñio.7 ibi.III.car. Ibi molin
7 III.ferui.Ibi.VI.uilti 7 IIII.bord cu.I.car.Ibi molin
redd.x.fot.7 VI.ac pti.Silua.II.q̃ lg.7 una q̃ lat.

Q̃do recep eps uatb.VI.lib.Modo.IIII.lib.
Idem eps ten ELENDVNE.T.R.E.geldb p.xxx.hid.
Tra.e.XII.car.De hac tra ft in dñio.xv.hidæ.7 ibi
.IIII.car.7 III.ferui.Ibi.xxv.uilti.7 XIIII.bord hñt
VII.car.Ibi.VI.molini reddt.xLII.fot.7 VI.denar.
7 Lx.ac pti.Pastura dimid leu lg.7 III.q̃rent lat.
7 xx.ac filuæ.
De hac tra ht un miles.I.hid 7 dimid.7 ht ibi.I.car.
Godric qui tenuit T.R.E.ñ potuit ab æccta feparari.

Q̃do eps recep uatb.xIIII.lib.Vat modo.xVIII.lib.
Ipfe eps ten CLIVE.T.R.E.geldb p.x.hid.Tra.e.v.car.
de ead tra ft in dñio.VI.hidæ 7 dimid.7 ibi.II.car.
7 III.ferui.Ibi.VII.uilti.7 III.cofcez.cu.II.car.
Ibi.xxx.ac pti.Silua.II.q̃ lg.7 una q̃ lat.
Q̃do eps recep uatb.III.lib.Modo.VI.lib.

Idem eps ten WEMBERGE.T.R.E.geldb p.XIX.hid.
Tra.e.x.car.De ead tra.IX.hidæ ft in dñio 7 ibi
III.car.7 VI.ferui.Ibi.XIX.uilti 7 XIII.bord cu.v.car.
Ibi molin redd.v.folid.7 xL.ac pti.Pastura dimid
leu lg.7 xv.q̃rent lat.De hac tra ten Richer.I.hid.
Q̃do recep eps uatb.xv.lib.Modo.xVIII.lib.

There was no resident priest, since Westwood remained part of Bradford parish and a chaplain from Bradford would have come over to Westwood to say mass and hear confessions.

The lower part of a cottage in Lower Westwood also seems to have been built about this time. When complete, it was probably the only two-storey stone house in the village. It may have been a courthouse: here the reeve would preside over the manor court, where disputes were settled and offences were tried by a jury of villagers. The reeve may even have lived in the building as caretaker.

The 13th century was a good time for country people and all over southern England rural populations increased. In AD 1249 the name *Avoneclive* appears in the cathedral records. Here, a generation or two later, Reynold of Cliff and Henry of Cliff ran the manor mill. It was an important part of village life, and although they were subject to the authority of the reeve and the manor court, the two men were entitled to pay their annual rent of 18 shillings and 7 sticks of eels direct to the cathedral.

By this time, the cathedral authorities were trying a new system of estate management. Instead of relying on a local reeve to manage their land, they started leasing out the whole manor estate. None of the first known lessees – Gilbert and James de Boulbek, Henry de Montfort and his brother Nicholas, Robert Waspray and his brother John – are known to have lived in Westwood. They all had other interests elsewhere and may have employed a local reeve to run the manor, just as the cathedral had done.

This was a boom time in farming and Westwood seems to have done fairly well. In AD 1334, when everyone was taxed at one-fifteenth of their income, the take from Westwood was 120 shillings – far more than that from any of the surrounding villages.

It was a time of change. As populations rose, more and more arable land was needed. The old pattern of small separate fields vanished as village lands were reorganised yet again. The plough-land was now concentrated into three huge open fields. Vanishing hedgerows and wildlife must have been a concern then, as now.

By the end of the Middle Ages, each villager farmed several long narrow strips of land which lay widely separated from each other in two of the

Opposite: Domesday Book entry in original Latin with English translation
(Reproduced by kind permission from Domesday Book volume 6 Wiltshire, (General Editor John Morris), published in 1979 by Phillimore & Co Ltd, Shopwyke Manor Barn, Chichester, West Sussex)

great open fields, one field always being left fallow. The reason for this scattering of the family lands is not clear. It may have been a deliberate arrangement, intended to give each family a fairer share of good and bad land, together with an equal risk of crop disease. On the other hand, it may just have been the result of generations of inter-marriage and inheritance.

The Black Death

After the boom came the bust. A series of bad harvests and epidemics of disease amongst sheep in the early years of the 14th century was followed by the Black Death.

The plague that swept across the Near East and Europe in 1348-9 killed up to a third of the population. The plague came again in 1368, and more people died. All over England, manor lords strove to keep their estates going by attracting peasants from stricken neighbouring settlements which were no longer economically viable. The shortage of agricultural labour enabled tenants to strike better bargains with their new lords than had been possible before the disaster, but even so there was not enough labour to go round. As was the case following the plagues in Roman Britain in the 4th century, land had to be turned over from arable to grazing, which required less in the way of manpower.

The effect of this in Westwood is clear. By AD 1377, the ploughed land on the manor demesne had shrunk to about half the area recorded in Domesday Book. In its place there was now grazing for 250 sheep. Some of the land reverted to woodland: Avoncliff wood was now twice the size it had been at Domesday. There were also two stone quarries.

Some people gained from the experience. Part of the old demesne land was now taken over by a new class of "free tenants" – peasants who had prospered and become rent-paying proprietors. One Westwood family held as many as 30 acres. Three other families had 15 acres each. The others had only a few acres apiece and had to go on working on the manor demesne, as their forefathers had done, in order to make ends meet.

Significantly, it is at this time that the manor records first distinguish between Nether Westwood and Over Westwood. Lye Green farm is also recorded as the home of John atte Legh. The new free tenants may thus have been farming the upper slopes between Upper and Lower Westwood, rather than the lower flatter lands where the three great open fields were.

A generation after the Black Death, there were only forty-five poll-tax payers in Westwood. This flat-rate tax (levied on everyone over the age of fourteen) was hard on poor rural communities, since the 4d demanded by the royal authorities from each adult was a large part of their disposable incomes. The actual adult population of Westwood may have been more than forty-five, since the tax collectors encountered a good deal of concealment and evasion, and before the Black Death the population may have been as much as seventy. Allowing for children under the age of fourteen, this gives a peak population figure for medieval Westwood of around two hundred, living in about thirty cottages divided between Nether Westwood with its chapel and court-house, Over Westwood, Avoneclive with its mill and eel-fishery, and outlying farms like Lye Green.

The "Lost Village" of Rowley

Halfway between Westwood and Farleigh lay the village of Rowley. Although it was originally part of the manor of Wingfield, some of its inhabitants farmed strips in the open fields of Westwood and must have worked on the cathedral's demesne here. By AD 1300, however, when Westwood was still just a chapelry in the parish of Bradford, Rowley was a separate parish with a church dedicated to St Nicholas.

In AD 1377, after the Black Death, there were fifty-three villagers at Rowley old enough to have to pay the poll tax - eight more than at Westwood. However, the difference may not reflect a larger population at Rowley. In 1334, less tax had been raised from Rowley than from Westwood. By 1377 there may just have been more tax-paying old people, and fewer children, at Rowley than at Westwood. A lack of young people would have been an ominous sign for a village, as it is today.

Whatever the reason, time was beginning to run out for Rowley. By 1428, the village had collapsed. There were less than ten adult parishioners. A century later, there was just one farm and a cottage standing in the overgrown village street. Today, there are just green fields where, if the light is right, you can still see the line of the old street and the low platforms where the houses once stood.

Renewed Prosperity

Gradually, the people of Westwood rebuilt their fortunes. Much of their wealth now came from sheep and cloth making had become a major industry in nearby Bradford and Trowbridge. The free tenants did best, since they paid their rent in money, rather than by working on the cathedral demesne. Whatever they earned over and above their rent, they could keep. In this way a hard-working family could advance its position.

These changed circumstances were recognised in far-away Winchester. The cathedral authorities now leased-out the right to farm their demesne land and to collect the rents due from the free tenants. The lessees of the manor – John Flower, Jon Atte Mulle and Henry Culverhouse – now lived in Westwood, possibly in a fairly modest house whose remains lie under the west wing of the present manor house.

It was Thomas Culverhouse, who leased the manor between about 1470 and 1485, who started a major rebuilding programme at the manor house. In 1480 he submitted an account to the Prior of St Swithun's cathedral, claiming a reduction in his rent because of the "new house built there (at Westwood) this year". He may also have added a new nave to the old thirteenth century chapel, which was by now dedicated to All Saints.

Later tenants extended the manor house still further. Perhaps the most important was Thomas Horton, who bought the lease in 1518. He was a successful merchant-clothier with commercial interests in Bradford, Trowbridge, Chippenham and London. He retired from business early and, seeking a quiet place near Iford where he had been born, came to Westwood.

Horton did not seek wealth from Westwood, but he sought status. The money he had accumulated from the booming wool trade not only allowed him to extend the manor house: it allowed him to add a great western tower to the nave of All Saints and later to build a side-chapel alongside the nave. Chapel and manor house together proclaimed the wealth, status and piety of the former cloth merchant.

Horton's extensions to the chapel were completed just in time for the Reformation. Under King Henry VIII, the church in England became the Church of England. At Winchester cathedral, the old monastic community was abolished and Westwood was confirmed as belonging to the new Dean and Chapter of the reformed cathedral. The new Book of Common Prayer was used in the chapel at Westwood by assistant curates who came over from Bradford, much as the medieval chaplains had done in earlier times.

As trade with still-Catholic Europe declined, the wool trade suffered. Most English cloth had been exported unfinished to the Low Countries, where it was dyed, stretched and sheared. Now the Belgian and French ends of the trade were in the hands of Catholic powers opposed to England. Towns like Bradford declined, and with them the surrounding villages where much of the spinning and weaving had been done in houses and cottages. It was to be another hundred years before matters improved.

The Civil War

By the time prosperity returned, the Civil War between King Charles I and Parliament had briefly torn England apart, setting father against son and brother against brother. At nearby Farleigh Castle, John Hungerford commanded a royalist garrison, while his half-brother Sir Edward led parliamentary troops against Lord Arundel's castle at Wardour and even went so far as to sign the death warrant which finally condemned King Charles to death on the scaffold.

Fierce battles were fought at Lansdown near Bath and at Roundway Down near Devizes in 1643 and for several years the opposing armies moved back and forth between London, Oxford and Bristol. It is unlikely that Westwood played much of a part in this, though some of the younger unemployed men may have taken the traditional way out and "gone for a soldier".

When the war ended in 1649, the people of Westwood were able to take stock of their position. The cathedral's demesne had shrunk to about half the total area of the manor. Much of its plough-land still lay in the three great open fields, but some of it had been enclosed with hedges to form small fields.

More significantly, the 190 acres of non-demesne land had been parcelled out into separate tenant farms, whose occupants were known as "copy-holders" since each held a copy of their written tenancy agreement. These new copyhold farms were still quite small in size - only nine of them were more than 10 acres.

Two of the larger farms were in Over Westwood. The eastern one (now known as Upper Farm) contained 40 acres, and a stone quarry. The western farm was slightly smaller: it contained about 34 acres and it also had a stone-quarry. In 1680, Zachary Walter rented it and added an imposing new residence to the old farmhouse: later known as Greenhill House, it is now called Well House.

Boom Time in Westwood

The 18th century saw a general improvement in conditions in Wiltshire. Although the army was involved in wars in France, America and India, there was peace at home.

The wool trade recovered, and on a new basis. The whole process, from spinning to finishing, was now carried out locally: cloth was no longer exported to France and Belgium to be finished.

At Avoncliff, the old corn mill was converted to a fulling mill some time between 1731 and 1763. The water wheel now worked heavy wooden trip-hammers, which pounded the newly woven cloth to thicken it. Dyeing and finishing the cloth may also have been carried out at the mill, or nearby in Bradford. However, the earlier stages of spinning and weaving could still be carried out in houses and cottages and many Westwood families probably augmented their incomes by this means.

Some of the money earned may have gone to the church of All Saints, where the nave was repaired and an ornate plasterwork ceiling was added. However, Avoncliff and Upper Westwood were some distance from All Saints, and many of the weavers, quarrymen and masons favoured the new teachings of John Wesley, who preached several times in the neighbourhood. Upper Westwood was beginning to develop a separate identity of its own.

This difference between the two settlements developed further with the growth of Bath as a fashionable spa town. Stone-quarrying became of more importance, and for the quarry-owners and workmen contacts with Bath and Bradford were more important than those with the old farming community of Lower Westwood, which remained grouped round the old church and manor-house.

Industrial development at Avoncliff continued apace. In 1791, John Moggeridge and Thomas Joyce converted the fulling mill to house machinery for finishing cloth – the first use of this process in west Wiltshire. A few years later they built a complex of weavers' houses (now known as Ancliff Square), so concentrating all stages of cloth-production at Avoncliff.

The change was not accomplished without pain. Within a year, Westwood had suffered its first recorded industrial injury. William Gibbence was only twelve years old when the new machinery in the cloth-mill trapped him and crushed him to death.

Nevertheless, the beginning of a canal linking Bath with Newbury and Reading held out the promise of further prosperity, allowing the easier transport of stone and cloth to where it was needed. In the event, the link did not become fully operational until 1810, but for a while the prospects seemed rosy.

The earliest detailed map of Westwood dates from 1792, just before the building of Ancliff Square. At first sight, the picture it gives of Westwood is reassuringly familiar. Most of the main roads and field-footpaths of today can be seen, together with many houses and cottages which are still in use. A closer look reveals some differences - survivals from an even older past. Standing out among the pattern of neatly hedged fields are vestiges of the three medieval open fields, with their long curving plough-strips.

Less than fifty houses can be seen on the map - about twenty in Lower Westwood, fifteen or so in Upper Westwood, two at Staples Hill and two at Lye Green. Avoncliff is not shown, but there must have been about eight or ten houses there. This suggests a population of about 350 people.

This estimate is confirmed by the first official census figures in 1801. By that time seventeen weavers' families had come to live in the newly built Ancliff Square and the total population of Westwood numbered 446 people. For all its recent industrialisation, Westwood was still a very small community.

Hard times again

The years of war with Napoleonic France severely disturbed the patterns of trade and industry built up in the previous century. For a while, the price of home-produced food soared. However, in 1815 the end of the war brought an agricultural slump as foreign produce became available again and the price of corn crashed.

The years after the war also saw much industrial unemployment. In 1835, the weavers' houses at Ancliff Square, which had fallen into disuse, were converted to a workhouse serving Bradford and the surrounding villages. By 1841 it was full of out-of-work weavers whose employers had been driven out of business by competition from the more mechanised cloth-mills of Yorkshire.

It was just as bad on the farms and many tenant farmers found themselves unable to pay their rents. The results of these years of poverty on Westwood are clear. While the population of England and Wales as a whole almost doubled in the years between 1801 and 1831, Westwood's population fell from 446 to 390: by 1841 it had fallen further to just 356 people, including children. Thereafter it rose slightly, but from then on the figure remained virtually static.

Even during these difficult years, however, there must have been some money about. Both the New Inn at Lower Westwood and the Cross Guns at Avoncliff were licensed houses in 1822, and may have been so for some time before then.

The existence of two inns reflected a real division in the community. Upper and Lower Westwood were not only geographically distinct: they were also divided by religion. The people of Upper Westwood and Avoncliff were predominantly Nonconformist. In 1863 the Wesleyan Methodists built a chapel in Upper Westwood: two years later the Baptists built themselves a chapel at the western end of Lower Westwood, well away from All Saints church.

In Lower Westwood, All Saints church had been repaired and refurbished, but there were still difficulties in finding suitable assistant curates who were prepared to live in the run-down Glebe Cottage which stood nearby. When Westwood finally achieved full parochial status in 1876, the church was re-dedicated to St Mary the Virgin and work began on an imposing new rectory: this was designed by two architects from Bristol, Charles Voysey and Frank Wills, both of whom were later to become famous for their buildings.

The long-standing connection with Winchester had finally ended in 1864, when the dean and chapter's estate at Westwood was sold to Mr C Tugwell, whose family had rented the estate since 1775. Westwood's link with the cathedral in Winchester had lasted for more than eight centuries, having begun twenty-three years before the Norman Conquest.

Modern times

Early in the 20th century a new means of travel opened new horizons for Westwood. The railway had come to Avoncliff in 1857 – but it had passed straight through! Although stone from the quarries was moved by rail by means of special sidings, it wasn't until 1906 that a station was built and trains stopped to pick up passengers.

A "snapshot" of Westwood at this time is provided by a plan made in 1911 for the sale of the manor estate. The Tugwell family was moving out after more than a century of tenancy and ownership.

Looking at the plan, it is surprising how little had changed since the end of the 18th century. The pattern of small fields laid out by the copyhold farmers in the 17th century had been regularised a little, though three extra large fields still preserved an echo of the open strip-fields of the medieval manor. At the west end of Lower Westwood there were now more houses and cottages round the school and Baptist chapel: there were a few more at the west end of Upper Westwood, too, and the lane leading down to Avoncliff had been realigned to make things easier for motor traffic. Even so, a time-traveller from the end of the 18th century, walking about Westwood at the beginning of the 20th century, would have recognised most of what he saw.

Throughout the ages, Westwood men had marched away to war. Some had returned, some had not. The Great War of 1914-18, however, had a far greater effect on local families than any previous war. Fourteen men never came home - a large number for a place as small as Westwood, where there can only have been about a hundred men of army age, many of whom were required to remain at home and farm the land.

Fewer Westwood men died in the Second World War, but that war was to have a dramatic effect on the shape of Westwood. Ninety-four new bungalows were built by the War Department to house families brought from the Midlands to work in Enfield's underground factory in the underground stone-quarries. Almost overnight, a new "Middle Westwood" was created in the fields between the old settlements of Upper and Lower Westwood and by 1951 the population of the parish had leaped to 915 - almost twice what it had been in 1931.

Since the end of the Second World War, further building has increased the size of Middle Westwood. Its existence marks a new chapter in the history of Westwood. For centuries, the people of Westwood worked on the land. Today, most of Westwood's residents find work away from the village – in Bradford, Trowbridge, Bath or Bristol. It is hard to picture how very empty the landscape looked just sixty years ago, before Middle Westwood was built. It is harder still to imagine the old Domesday manor of just fifteen families which is so proudly recorded on the gateway to the parish church.

Westwood has a long history and the landscape around it has changed many times. Prairie-farming and hedgerow removal, agricultural set-aside and local authority housing quotas are just modern versions of the forces that shaped our village across the last two millennia. No doubt further changes lie ahead of us. In looking to the future, Westwood can be proud of its past.

Brian K Davison

Westwood: Then and Now

THERE IS MARKED difference between the village today and that of late Victorian England due to the major changes in social conditions, housing, employment, schooling and healthcare which have taken place over the last hundred years. Direct comparisons, substantiated by firm facts, are difficult to identify, but if we retrace our steps a further twenty years to the 1881 census we do at least have a reasonable basis on which to make some very simple comparisons. Today's data was obtained from a very simple demographic survey undertaken in the village in the early part of 2000 in which some 65% of the village participated.

The 1881 population, in theory, was 509, of whom 123 lived in the Bradford-on-Avon Workhouse at Avoncliff (now The Old Court), which (while technically part of the Parish) had more in common with Bradford-on-Avon, so for the purpose of this article the Workhouse data has been ignored. Thus, the population proper of Westwood was 386 of whom 228 had been born in the village, 28 in Bradford-on-Avon and a further 23 in the surrounding villages. Those of the remainder who were born in England gave their birthplaces as follows:

Bath, Melksham, Swindon and Westbury	68
Bristol/Somerset	21
London, Home Counties & the South East	8
West Country /Midlands	4

A further six people were born outside England, one in Wales, one in Scotland (Aberdeenshire),two in the East Indies (the local Vicar and his wife, Basil and Ella Babington), one in Brussels (Harriet Rooke the younger sister of Juliet Rooke the owner of Iford Manor, who had been born in Essex) and Thomas Hazell (aged 8) whose birthplace was recorded as the USA (however, the rest of the family were born in Westwood!) How or why people, born in such far flung places came to live in Westwood makes for interesting speculation and what is the story behind Thomas Hazell or was this a mistake in the recording process?

The table below shows the population spread, by age, of the Village in 1881 and compares it to details abstracted from the 2000 survey; the small size of this sample precludes specific comparisons.

Population Spread by Age

	1881	2000
Pre-School	19	28
Primary	94	63
Secondary	48	65
16-20	38	17
21-30	53	49
31-40	56	75
41-50	34	123
51-60	31	151
61-70	6	112
71 +	7	100

The population of modern day Westwood, including The Old Court, is 910, as quoted in the local electoral register. The most dramatic change between 1881 and 2000 is that very few people are now actually born in the village. In 1881 the figure was some 60% of the inhabitants, while today there are only twenty or so, as most local children are now born in the Bath or Trowbridge Hospitals. So where were the current villagers born? While a goodly number have local roots - Bradford and the surrounding area - the majority were born literally throughout the length and breadth of England from Cornwall to Northumbria. The picture is one of a mobile population typical of our modern society and very typical of a Village like ours, located as it is in beautiful countryside relatively close to major urban areas - Bath, Bristol and Swindon - and within relatively easy travelling distance of London. We are very close to the major rail and road networks with Bristol, Cardiff and London Airports all readily accessible so it is hardly surprising that the village was an attractive proposition for developers; hence the influx of newcomers in the eighties and nineties. The first major influx took place during World War 2 with the development of the Enfield Works, and since then people have moved here for a variety of reasons:

- job relocation, promotion / transfer
- to establish a business
- retirement
- to move out of an urban environment
- the reasonable cost of housing
- to be near families
- they liked the area
- they wanted a pleasant environment in which to bring up children

Also of interest are the wonderfully diverse places in which people were born outside the United Kingdom and Ireland and this list, if anything, reflects clearly how the mobility of society has changed throughout this century. The 'Foreign Parts' we know of are: Australia, Ceylon, Italy, Singapore, Barbados, Denmark, Japan, South Africa, Buenos Aries, Eire, Kenya, Teheran, Burma, Germany, Malta, Zimbabwe, Brazil, India, New Zealand.

The working population in 1881 was 152, the bulk of whom would have been employed within the Parish. The main employers were:

The Stone Quarry
  1 Engineer
  13 Stone Masons
  1 Carter
  27 Labourers

Farming
  4 Farmers
  2 Shepherds
  35 Labourers
  2 Dairy Workers

Domestic Service: 21

Cloth Mill: 16

The Parish also had its own Dressmakers, Baker, Innkeeper, General Labourers and a Railway Worker. Other occupations listed included 2 Landowners, the Schoolmaster and SchoolMistress, Rector, Grocer,

Carpenters and Woodcutters. There was only one body, at the time of the census, who was classed as "out of work".

As is to be expected, there is little in common between the occupations of Victorian England and today. The most notable change being the decline in agriculture with less than ten people now engaged in this sector and there is indeed no longer a working farm in the Parish. The occupations of the rest of the village are as diverse as their places of birth and the survey identified in excess of eighty different current and past occupations. Some of the more unusual/interesting jobs referred to include, Coastguard, Gunmaker, Codebreaker, BBC Radio Producer, Film Producer, Airline Pilot, Firefighter, Mountain Guide and Watchmaker, to mention but a few. With all the skills available, it would seem that the Village could be as self-supporting now as it was in 1881.

Sheila Biles, Terry Biles, Sue Woods

The Tithe Map of the Parish of Westwood, Wiltshire, 1843

THIS IS A HAND-DRAWN map kept in the County Record Office in Trowbridge. It is large, measuring about five feet by four and all the dwellings and areas of land marked on it are numbered. It comes with a roll of parchment pages which give details of the land and property, recording who owns what with a brief description - house, cottage, tenement; arable, pasture, orchard.

The final column shows the amount of Tithe due from each owner and at the end is the amount Westwood paid the Rector each year. This is called the Gross Tithe and in 1843 it amounted to £190. The Parish also paid £1.8s. (£1.40) to the Rector of Hungerford Farleigh in Berkshire.

When this map was published there were approximately seventy-five dwellings in Westwood Parish and it is notable how few of the land and property owners occupied, or worked, what they owned. Most appears to have been let to others who paid rent from which the Tithe came. William Dyke rented what is now 82 Lower Westwood, which is described as "House and Beer Shop".

Some of the landowners' names have a current resonance: Samuel Bythesea, William Dauncey, the Kennet and Avon Canal Company (who owned a cottage), the Earl Manvers (who owned the wood we know as Becky Addy, but which was then called just Addy Wood), Henry Shrapnell, George Clutterbuck Tugwell (who, with Maria Joyce and the Dean and Chapter of Winchester, owned some thirty-six properties and fields), Richard Windo and John and Frederick Yerbury.

There were fields called Little Hobbs, Great Hobbs and Housels. William, Thomas, John and Mary Hobbs all had dwellings. And Richard Windo owned what are marked as plots 234 and 235 on the Map and he is recorded as having let plot 233, a tenement, to Joseph Hobbs.

Ros Bartlett

A Farming Story

ONE HUNDRED YEARS ago our village was an almost empty rural scene of green fields and hedgerows, cut through by the parallel courses of Upper and Lower Westwood roads with their thin scattering of cottages and farm dwellings. Today housing estates cover most of the land between these two roads, where once cattle grazed. In spite of this, we are one of the lucky villages in that, by and large, we are still green. How much more pleasant to look out on pasture and meadow, as we mostly do, than on acres and acres of combinable crops as far as the eye can see.

Back in 1900, Westwood was an estate-owned village, as it had been for centuries past, until the estate was carved up at auction in 1911, thus creating a community of small-holdings, while the copy held properties of Green hill and Upper Westwood farms passed into private ownership.

In this chapter I shall try to describe the fortunes of these farms, many no longer in existence, as well as new enterprises of the last decade or two. There are numerous gaps in the story where research has failed me or where I have deliberately left out certain farms, those, for example, that are, quite literally, borderline cases. The reader will also be aware that many fields inside the parish boundary are owned by farmers or businessmen who live outside the parish, some as far away as Frome or Bath, and these farms go unmentioned too, with the exception of Upper Westwood Farm.

Records are scant on this topic. I am therefore enormously grateful to those people who allowed me to draw on their memories, and hope that nothing too egregious will be found in the retelling. I am also indebted to Mike Hawke for lending me vital documents and especially to Mick Rahilly for allowing me to reproduce his entertaining account of Tommy Welch and life at Limes Farm Cottage.

The farms fall into four categories, listed alphabetically within their groups: Past Farms, Present Farms, Nursery Farms and Hobby Farms.

Past Farms
Avon Villa Farm (1830-1971) has interesting origins connected to Ancliff

Square, which in 1830 was a workhouse. The villa was built to house the master of the workhouse while inmates farmed the adjoining fields to provide for their sustenance.

When the institution closed in 1914 (to become a hotel) the farm was taken over by the Avoncliff Flock Mill, which then belonged to Farleigh Hungerford Estate. Today the mill buildings are private dwellings.

The farm and villa passed into single ownership in 1926 and gradually grew from 12 to 60 acres, plus 20 acres of woodland (Becky Addy). The 60 acres were spread between Turleigh, Avoncliff and Westwood. 30 Ayrshire milking cows were herded daily to and from one of these points and the farmer's milk round between Avoncliff and Turleigh came on top – hard graft to most of us but an accepted way of life then.

There is little good timber in Becky Wood, mainly small Sycamore, small Ash, Hazel and similar low-grade woods useful for fencing posts or firewood. Thirty years ago, 10 acres at the canal end were cleared for pasture.

In 1971 the farmer retired keeping the villa, now a B & B, the 3-acre field by the river below it, the Teazel's site and the car park. His other Westwood acres were sold to 'Leigh Green Farm'.

Greenhill Farm (Well House) Grade II*
Originally named 'Well House', Greenhill was one of the copyholdings of the Westwood Manor Estate, with 160 acres of pasture and arable, mostly lying south of the house as far as Lower Westwood Road and west to the Iford fork.

George Hazell, Senior, ploughing the field opposite Well House in the early 1900s.

The handsome late 17th/early 18th century house which is situated on the north side of Upper Westwood Road once stood free of its gabled extensions which were built in the 1900's, at separate stages. A matching wing was added in order to restore the symmetry of the house.

I have been unable to piece together the story around 1911. We know that the farm was put up for sale as a 'Valuable Freehold Dairy Farm including Stabling for four horses: Yard; Barn; Piggeries and Cow House for over a dozen cows; Rick Yard, etc.'

At some point, Alfred Hazell, either as tenant or owner occupied Greenhill. A prominent farming family of the day, as were the Marshes before, Alfred had nine children and countless grandchildren who would come visiting and tear around the panelled rooms playing 'hide and seek'.

There were five Hazell sons. One was a beer retailer at the village off-licence. His wife would scrub the beautiful flagstones. When customers came calling, she would shout at customers wishing to buy cigarettes, "Take what you want and leave the money on the counter 'cos I'm down on me knees!" Two of the sons moved into Upper Farm and two more were sent to work at Parsonage Farm at Winsley. In the days when family cohesion meant more than economic prosperity, father Alfred built a row of cottages (111 – 114 Upper Westwood Road) for his sons' retirement. There is a splendid photograph of the bearded patriarch among his brood taken outside Upper Farm on the occasion of his daugher's wedding. Several members of the Hazell family, including Alfred, lie buried in our little cemetery.

A Hazell family wedding group outside Upper Farm in the 1920s

Greenhill had been a dairy farm under the Hazells. When war came and a large acreage was requisitioned for housing, the presiding owners sold up and left the country in disgust. Where once was a large orchard, in front of the house, there is a much reduced but exquisite formal garden to the left of which is the original potting and apple store ('The Long House').

Under its new owners, Greenhill has reverted to its original name, 'Well House'.

'Haygrove Farm'
Situated half way through the village on the side of Lower Westwood Road, 'Haygrove Farm', now a nursery site, was one of the smallholdings to emerge from the land sale of 1911. The farmhouse, now divided into two dwellings, stands next to a barn by the road opposite 'The Laurels'.

In approximately 1915, the son of the publican at the 'New Inn' acquired the 24-acre farm and set up a small mixed livestock business. An energetic man, Mr Holdway kept cattle and three carthorses. He put up a pigsty, built a poultry incubator with his own hands and worked a two-acre vegetable allotment. With four small mouths to feed, he would turn his hand to anything that would bring in a bit of money. When 'Westview', the farm next door, fell into disrepair (the three elderly occupants were not coping) Holdway mended its walls and ditches and generally saw to its upkeep. In 1929 his elder son Jack became the new tenant farmer there.

Mr Holdway gave up his farm after World War II, his four children having gone their separate ways. There were further owners but latterly the farm was not kept up and today The Haygrove land has been put to other uses.

The Limes Farm – now 'Limes Farm Cottage' (by Mick Rahilly)
My wife and I, along with our five children aged 15-4, moved into The Old Malt House in 1958, then called 'The Limes'. The farm was owned by Tommy Welch and his wife. The extent of his land was the two fields to the North and East of 'The Old Malt House', and the field across the lane leading to Upper Westwood, now occupied by Linden Crescent.

Their accommodation was distinctly primitive, consisting of one long room, which now forms the upper floor of 'Limes Farm Cottage', sub-divided into three – a living room, bedroom and kitchen.

The kitchen contained a cooking-stove, a fridge and a sink with a cold tap – the sole water supply. The 'sanitation' comprised an Elsan in a 'bogey hole' under the outside staircase on the East end of the building, which was a problem for Mrs Welch who had severe arthritis.

The ground floor of the building, now the kitchen, dining room and drawing room of 'Limes Farm Cottage', contained a byre and a stable for Polly – Tommy's milk-float horse.

I cannot remember how many cows he ran, but they were sufficient for him to provide a milk round to the greater part of the village, which was considerably smaller in terms of inhabitants in those days.

He originally conducted a 'traditional' round, with milk churns and dippers (1 pint and half-pint) in his milk float pulled by Polly. My second son, Brian, who died 5 years ago, occasionally accompanied him on his rounds, as did Malcolm Fowler who lives in Friary Close.

It was said that during the Christmas rounds when Tommy, who was universally popular, was invited into various (numerous!) homes for "a dram", Polly could find her own way home without any assistance from him!

Eventually, he was forced to bottle his milk – with somewhat strange results, as his bottle washing equipment was fairly rudimentary.

Peggy and I, on application to some "authority" or other, were granted the right to buy our milk by the jug "on an ex-farmhouse door basis" in their jargon, which was a great relief!

In mid 1961 Tommy decided to "pack it in" in his wording, and move back to Dorset, from where he originally came, to join his brother who farmed near Weymouth.

My wife, Peggy, and I first bought the farm buildings and a small strip of land to the North of the North wall of the 'Malt House' (which now belongs to Simon and Amanda Relph) and subsequently at an auction, attended by only 4 people apart from Tommy and the auctioneer, bought the North and East fields for which Tommy had obtained outline planning permission for building, mainly to prevent any building surrounding us. The planning permission lapsed after roughly 7 years and we made no attempt to renew it.

In September 1962 we obtained Development Permission to convert the barn and so-called flat above it into a cottage. This work was carried out by Mr E J Stow of Southwick and, after occupation by a number of tenants, including Mr & Mrs Preddy (who took over the milk delivery business), was sold to Derrick & Mary Cook.

I still own the North and East fields. The 5-acre field was not sold at the auction mentioned above, to Tommy's dismay, but was subsequently bought by a building firm who built Linden Crescent and Tommy then appeared in our yard in a posh new car, wearing a posh new suit!

Payne's Farm 1922–1982

This small farm of approximately 11 acres lay at the far end of Iford Fields on the site of the present bungalow.

Mr Newton John Payne bought the land in 1922 and built two small asbestos dwellings – one for himself and his wife, the other for his wife's sister and husband who worked for GWR (Great Western Railway).

Initially, Payne farmed chickens. He had two poultry houses built, one with a "state of the art" battery unit. Behind the two bungalows there also stood a broody shed and apple orchard. Later, he built six pigsties.

After the outbreak of World War II, Payne turned approximately half of his land into vegetable production using Land Girls and POW labour. When the war was over he put up a domed shed, still seen today, for use as a farm shop – an early example. He sold greengroceries, apples and eggs but no ham joints: the pigs were sent for slaughter. Some villagers still remember him driving around delivering his produce in Westwood and various hostelries in Bradford on Avon.

Mr Payne and his farmshop were so well known in the area that Iford Fields became known as Payne's Lane – even letters so addressed would reach their destination.

Payne retired in the late 1960s. When the farm was sold in 1982, soon after his death, the fields were bought separately and the buildings (most of them by then falling apart) were cleared to make way for the present bungalow and garden.

Westview Farm 1920-2000

We were sorry to see 'Westview' close down earlier this year with the departure of the last milking herd in Westwood and the owner's retirement. 'Westview' was the last traditional farm owned in the village.

Situated opposite the public telephone box on the Lower Westwood Road, 'Westview' was a county farm, that is to say, Council owned in the 1920s and tenant-farmed until the late 1970s when the incumbent bought the farm off the County Council. He farmed 60 acres and 50 head of dairy cattle. The farmhouse seems a familiar relic of the old council style, that is, red brick and green trimming.

'Westview' has an attractive acreage of fields, a copse, a stream and a little bluebell wood, which attracts the local deer population.

The dry herd we see temporarily installed is owned elsewhere and half the land has now been sold or let for grazing.

FARMS TODAY

Hillside Farm

A five-acre farm lives in deepest seclusion off Upper Westwood Road at the western end of the village. Some might argue that the activity is too insignificant to justify the term for the owner does not farm. He is busy with his profession in the field of music. So the grass grows, the haymakers come, the owner keeps his views and others do the work. The farm may be insignificant but the lifestyle is not.

Leigh Green Farm 1890–

Leigh Green derives from Lye Green, an 'old settlement' (*Victoria County History, Vol. II*) lying off the Upper Westwood Road, half way to Jones Hill. We know there was a 16th century granary works – 'Flintstones' used to be three quarry workers' cottages – and presumably some sort of farming activity was present to support the enterprise. However, there appear to be no links with today's farm, other than an old track (today a footpath) thought to have been used for hauling stones or returning quarrymen, which runs through Leigh Green fields.

The Lye Green district was not part of Westwood Manor Estate but today lies within the Westwood Parish boundary.

The present farm building, recently expanded, was built in 1890 by Mr Godwin who is also said to have built 'Limes Farm Cottage'. The land consists of 85 acres, mostly pasture, approximately 70 acres of which lie inside the parish boundary. This includes, (on the north side of the farm), 'Becky Addy Wood' as far as the canal and the fields, west to the swing bridges, two fields on the south side of the Lower Westwood Road and a large acreage near Budgens.

'Leigh Green', previously a dairy farm, has kept 50 beef cattle under its present owner who disposed of them on his retirement and now keeps a very small number of beef.

In 1972 his daughter, working from the same premises, opened a DIY stable with capacity for 25 horses. For those of you, like me, surprised to hear the term, a "DIY Stable" (unlike livery stables) has facilities only for renting out. In other words, the renter does all the training, exercising and mucking-out herself. The facilities include stabling, a sand school (area of sand for training) which can be seen by the farm buildings on your way to Jones Hill, a jump field further towards Jones Hill on the right, 80 acres of grazing plus hay supplies. 'Clients' are mostly hacking horses and the occasional thoroughbred training for show jumping or cross-country events. The stable owner is proud of her tally: 107 horses have passed through the books since 1972.

Manor Farm

We have one stretch of arable in Westwood, a 60 acre tenant farm owned by the National Trust since the 1950's. The original farm stood on a site opposite to the Manor, the present Manor Cottage by Farleigh Hungerford Lane being once the old farmhouse. I understand that its beautiful farm buildings, then still in use, were shamefully pulled down by the Trust because yard smells were unwelcome outside the manor gates. A nearby cattle shed was also destroyed 15 years later – a suspected arson attack.

The farm comprises the acres south of the manor retained by the owner when he put the estate up for sale in 1911. There was mixed farming until two years' ago. Now the cows have gone and only crops are grown, mainly cereal.

Walkers will have noticed the wide margins edging the crop fields. Margins are left uncultivated, to comply with Brussels' regulations to reduce grain production by 10% due to surpluses. Trust and tenant plan to manage these verges as a conservation project by growing a type of meadow grass which they hope will encourage the return of the small species in the food chain.

While the official footpath will continue its direct route through the fields to Stowford, plans are afoot to place signs suggesting that walkers might like to try out the alternative and more pleasurable "circumambulatory" route which, incidentally, takes only three minutes more to walk than the footpath – I've tried it.

Upper Westwood Farm (Grade II)

When the farmer and milking herd went two years ago, it appeared that Westwood's most high profile farm had closed. This is not exactly the case. Most know but some don't, that the farmer was not the owner but the

Manager and that Upper has been in absentee ownership for many years. The farm premises now stand grievously empty, decisions pending the result of planning applications. The owner says he would not have another milking herd, explaining that his fields lie off a road all in one direction, away from the milking shed, which itself is ill-situated at the busy end of the village, making the daily milk drive long and problematic for the cows.

The situation would only get worse in future with the increasing number of cars in Westwood. Meanwhile, the fields are rented out for grass-keep and some 200 beef cattle have been shipped in from elsewhere, following a winter experiment involving Welsh mountain sheep about which more later.

Upper Farm, Westwood (Tony Hawtin).

To get to the history: a former copyholding, Upper Farm, (with its imposing mostly 17th century farmhouse), was occupied by the prolific Marsh family from 1851 to 1900. In the 1911 land sale, the particulars quoted the property as, 'A Superior Farmhouse [and] Capital range of buildings including stone-built Barn, Cow-houses, Stabling, Yards and Piggeries.' Later, Alfred Hazell lived there until he died in 1926. His son, Albert, next took residence, and in 1939 sold the property to the father of the present owner.

The farm came with 112 acres, 32 dairy cows and a bull, three cartmares and 50 head of poultry. More acres and cattle were purchased bringing the complement to 124 acres and 60 cows. The herd had to go when BSE regulations and depressed milk prices destroyed the livestock market.

The farm has surely impinged on the lives of villagers more than any other in Westwood. Quite apart from the pleasure of seeing (not too closely) the farmhouse with its interesting architectural features as you enter Upper Westwood village, one is (or was) conscious of Upper as a highly visible working farm, and the source of many an animal story, some amusing (in retrospect!), others utterly fraught. I should tell you a few of these:

About 25 years ago a villager was amazed one morning on opening his curtains to see five cows flat on their backs with rigid legs pointing upwards. These unfortunate creatures had been electrocuted in a thunderstorm when sheltered under an Elm whose stump can still be seen in the field in front of the farmhouse.

Then there was the story in 1991, when a couple of cows went 'berserk' and trampled a clutch of gardens in Upper Westwood before charging down the hill to Avoncliff where they were finally rounded up.

Thirdly, those sheep mentioned earlier: the owner of the farm wanted to graze off the tufted autumn grass to make for a better Spring growth. A livestock agent suggested sheep for the purpose and sourced some Welsh mountain sheep, which duly arrived in January 1998. Unfortunately, the fencing was woefully inadequate for this free-ranging breed; sheep eventually broke out and invaded the village, much to the dismay of the garden-proud and embarrassment of the farmer.

Again, there is an awful and most recent story about the fatal encounter between a peaceable old collie dog and agitated mother cows in one of the Upper fields. All of us who walk our dogs there sympathise with the owner who drew the short straw.

And lastly, if ever a vision were needed, let it be the rescue of Upper farmhouse before it crumbles irreparably.

NURSERY FARMS

Downside Nursery Farm

The story of this family nursery business started in 1968 with 13 acres of pasture at the western extremity of Upper Westwood purchased for a horticultural production. The success of this venture allowed for the purchase of a further 50 scattered acres and 40 beef cattle. Then came the collapse of the vegetable market in the 1980s due to imported goods and high-tech mass production in the eastern counties. At that stage the farm propped up the nursery while it converted from vegetables to ornamentals, mainly annual bedding plants. It turned out a shrewd move, the trade was receptive and local people came in numbers to buy.

Then, in a further twist, came BSE and the demise of the beef side of the business. The nursery side did not falter, introducing hardy perennials on which basis it is expanding now, in tandem with the bedding operation.

Today, 'Downside' has four glass houses and two brand new sophisticated polytunnels nearing completion, one with five bays, the other with nine bays divided into two climate zones. The sprinkler systems, now manual, will shortly be fully automated.

The momentum has been impressive, with one temporary reversal during the 1987 storm when the glass roofs were lost. Now, 'Downside' has an enviable customer base, supplying 80% of their business to the trade. There are four full-time employees including two family members and part-time seasonal workers increasing to a total of 14 employees during the height of the season.

Haygrove Nursery

In the 1970s a well-known Trowbridge pharmacist with an interest in horticulture bought land of the former Haygrove Farm to provide his family with a nursery business. Situated at the top end of Farleigh Hungerford Lane in the dip to the north of the Glebe (Church Fields), the nursery had small beginnings growing and selling strawberries. Having borne fruit the business multiplied, so to speak, with the introduction in 1989 of bedding and pot plants and flower crops which is the main business of the nursery today.

There are two large glass houses and three polytunnels, these last currently out of use during construction work.

Haygrove Nursery is still a 'one-man operation' supplying only the wholesale trade, on an axis from Gloucestershire to Yeovil. With so few hands, the owner relies on his mechanised potting machine and sprinkler system to free him for delivery trips. It sounds, and is, hard work needing many a 4 a.m. start to the day.

HOBBY FARMS

We have a few pocket farms in the area with an interest in the rare breed business.

One of the examples is a goat enclosure, today filled with 13 mixed nanny goats being cared for life, 5 cockerels and 15 hens.

It was not always like this. The owners' interest in rearing goats began 21 years ago when goat's milk was not readily available and needed in the family for dietary reasons. The interest led to breeding the rare English goat, registered as the Avonwood herd. This Spring the herd was cruelly devastated by theft of the stud goat and all the billies. Given the time and energy it would take to rebuild the herd to pedigree standard, the project has been abandoned and the owners, who after all these years have goats in the blood, still carry on but with rescue work only.

Another rare breed in the village is the Wiltshire Horn, a clever sheep that does not need shearing and is good to eat. The programme started in 1998 with registration of the herd with the Wiltshire Horn Society. A pedigree ram gets 'hired' for six weeks in the Autumn and all lambs are registered, two of which this year were rams, one being reared for breeding, the other to be slaughtered for meat.

So that is it. In the last century Westwood has turned from a farming community into a residential community but without losing its rural integrity. It is true that there have been minor breaches in conservation areas and one must hope that this will not become a trend.

The fields we see are by and large those our predecessors saw but there is a difference. We now have managed hedgerows, sometimes with odd results and I understand that those which have disappeared completely are destined for renewal. Thanks to Brussels, we have the set-asides and lay-down policy drawing village comments like, "nice for the bunnies" or, "just a load of weeds". Farmers are becoming environmentalists either because they want to or have to, or it pays them to do so. This may be bearing results already because we do see some marvellous meadows on our doorstep.

But gone are the cows and the familiar tankers bearing down on Westwood every lunch hour to collect the milk from Upper and Westview farms. 'In' are rural buses (God bless them), removal vans, Tesco delivery vans and the 'Jones's' with their 4 x 4s. But you are still just as likely to collide with a loaded tractor though the driver is probably on contract hire, as is much of the labour in the fields. There is a tendency for farmers to pool their resources to buy expensive machinery and take turns with it. There are a few DIY farmers left. Today you can have a farm and not be there: somebody is hired to do the lot. And that is why Westwood is no more a farming community.

Jean Stevenson

The Last Village Blacksmith

AT THE ENTRANCE to Orchard Close off the narrow part of Lower Westwood, there used to be the village blacksmith, complete with 'spreading chestnut tree'. He was Colin Windo and his death was reported in the Wiltshire Times of 20 January 1940:

Colin Windo.

"By the death of Mr. Colin Windo, which took place on Thursday, 11 January, a familiar figure is removed from the village of Westwood, where for well over forty years he was the village blacksmith. Aged 68 years, in his younger days he was a popular sportsman and entered into the social life of the village with zest. He was captain of the village cricket team for many years and well known as a keen bowler. The funeral took place on Monday at St. Mary's Church, Westwood, when the esteem in which Mr Windo was held was shown by the large number of floral tributes and the large attendance of villagers and friends."

ARTHUR PADFIELD, who grew up at Dogkennel Farm at Iford, remembers bringing his father's horses up to the Westwood smithy to be shod. And JUNE DOUGLAS, who now lives in a bungalow built on the ground where the smithy stood, has dug up many fascinating objects, including horseshoes, in her garden.

WILTS, BORDERS OF SOMERSET.

THE WESTWOOD MANOR ESTATES,

Near BRADFORD-ON-AVON,

with Station at Avon Cliff Halt almost adjoining, 1 mile from Bradford-on-Avon and Freshford,
and within seven miles of the City of Bath.

Particulars and Conditions of Sale

IN NUMEROUS LOTS ranging from

$\frac{1}{4}$ of an Acre to 112 Acres

INCLUDING

Dairy and Mixed Farms, Building Sites, Cottages, Small Holdings, &c.

MESSRS. NICHOLAS

IN CONJUNCTION WITH MESSRS.

POWELL & POWELL, Ltd.

Will sell the above, at

The Auction Mart, Quiet Street, Bath,

On Wednesday, July 12th, 1911,

At 3.30 o'clock precisely.

Copies of these Particulars and Conditions of Sale, with Plan, may be obtained of Messrs. CAMERON, KEMM & Co., Solicitors, Gresham House, Old Broad Street, London, E.C.; of Messrs. POWELL AND POWELL, Ltd., Estate Agents, Old Bond Street, Bath; or of the Auctioneers, Messrs. NICHOLAS,
43, PALL MALL, LONDON, S.W., STATION ROAD, READING, and NEWBURY.

BRADLEY & SON, LTD., READING.

The Great Land Sale of 1911

Background

Westwood is generally a difficult village on which to research history because, for nearly a thousand years, its owner lived outside the County of Wiltshire and detailed records of village business were not stored locally. For instance, in *The Victoria History of the Counties of England, Wiltshire Volume 7* which deals with the Hundreds of Bradford, Melksham and Pottern with Cannings, Westwood has nine mentions, mostly brief. Wingfield, on the other hand, has no less than thirty such mentioned, together with over seven pages of dedicated historical account. Shame!

The earliest known news of Westwood dates from 983 when King Ethelred (he who is said to have been unready) granted land to his servant, Aelfnoth. But in about 1020 his Queen Emma gave us to the Bishop of Winchester. In the Domesday Book of 1086 we are still assigned to the said Bishop. This, of course, is the reason why we have a tithe barn and our neighbouring villages do not. We paid our tithes to Winchester. Others in the Bradford Hundred took their tithes to Bradford and the fine tithe barn there protected them.

By 1775 the Tugwell family were leasing the Manor and lands from the Chapter at Winchester. In 1861 the Manor and lands were transferred to the Ecclesiastical Commissioners of England. They, in turn, sold most, but not all to the Tugwells on at least four separate occasions between February 1867 and September 1901.

The Sale

In 1911 the Tugwells sold the Manor House to Mr E G Lister who was a member of the Diplomatic Service. He was not a farmer and decided that the lands to the south and east of Farleigh Lane (basically the land now owned by The National Trust with the Manor House) were sufficient for his modest needs. Accordingly, Mr Henry William Tugwell of Crow Hall, Bath, placed the sale of his remaining lands in the hands of Messrs. Nicholas, Auctioneers of Pall Mall, London and Messrs Powell & Powell Limited,

Estate Agents of Old Bond Street, Bath. The land on offer extended from Haygrove Plantation in the south to the River Avon in the north and from Staples Hill eastwards to beyond the turning to Elms Cross.

The sale catalogue is a glossy affair and contains a large scale and very detailed map of the village. I have traced two copies, one in Winchester Cathedral Library, the other in the County Records Office at Trowbridge. The latter copy is particularly interesting because someone has pencilled in the prices realised at auction and indicated which lots may not have been sold because they are unmarked.

The sale was of great interest in Westwood because nearly everyone was about to change their landlord and, if not their employer, then their employer's landlord. Two who would have then been in their early teens and remembered the sale well were Jack Batterick and Bert Hobbs. Jack could recite who bought what like a catechism, stumbling only on the unsold lots. Bert, being a stone quarryman of Upper Westwood, was more selective in his memories but had a lot to say about the disputes and doubts which resulted from the lots remaining unsold.

Some parts of the village remained outside the sale. As the Tugwells were selling-up, the most likely reason was that these lands had been retained by the Ecclesiastical Commissioners in 1861 or had already been sold by Mr Tugwell. These included:-

Shrub Cottage	Possibly owned by Iford Manor
The Cemetery	
The land on which	Linden Crescent
	Orchard Close
	The Laurels
	Westwood House
	86A, 86B, 86C and 86D Lower Westwood
	The Malt House
	Limes Farm Cottage
	The New Inn
	47 to 56 Lower Westwood
	81 to 86 Lower Westwood
	The Churchyard
	Westwood Manor and Orchard (sold to Mr Lister)
	The Old Vicarage and The Rectory

The field in which 101 Upper Westwood and Cottles
Stables now stand
107 & 108 Upper Westwood and land
Avon Cottage (Canal Company property?)
The Old Court, Avoncliff and land

The field opposite the reservoir where John Blake
built his stables was not all included in the sale.
Nor was any property at Lye Green included.

We tend to think that Westwood has developed a lot and become very
urbanised. Certainly, it has ceased to be the sheep farming and stone
quarrying community of ninety years ago. But note how many of the lots
below have changed not at all in their use in 1911.

The Lots

Lot No.	Auction Description	Date of Deeds	Present Status in Westwood	Remarks
1	Garden Ground	14/05/1869	Garden opposite the house of Staples Hill	No change today. The far-western lot in the sale
2	Freehold Building Estate, "Great Down"	14/05/1869	Field to the north of Staples Hill	No change today
3	Freehold Building	14/05/1869	The triangle of land now containing Housels Field, Downside Nurseries and 143 to 146 Upper Westwood	Some let to Mr S E Marsh
4	An Excellent Freehold Building Site	23/02/1867 and a Statutory Declaration	Field opposite Iford Manor east of Housels Field	No change today
5	An Exceptionally Attractive Property	14/05/1869	Shrub Down. The south-facing slope from Staples Hill	No change today
6	Valuable Accommodation Land	4/05/1869 & 23/02/1867	Fields to the east of The Old Court along the bank of the Avon	Some let to Mr S E Marsh Still agricultural
7	A Capital Freehold Property	23/02/1867 and a Statutory Declaration	Avoncliff Wood north of Downside Nurseries	Some let to Mr S E Marsh Still in agricultural use
8	Building or Accommodation Land	14/05/1889	Fields along the river bank south east of Iford Manor	Let to Mr John Marsh Still agricultural

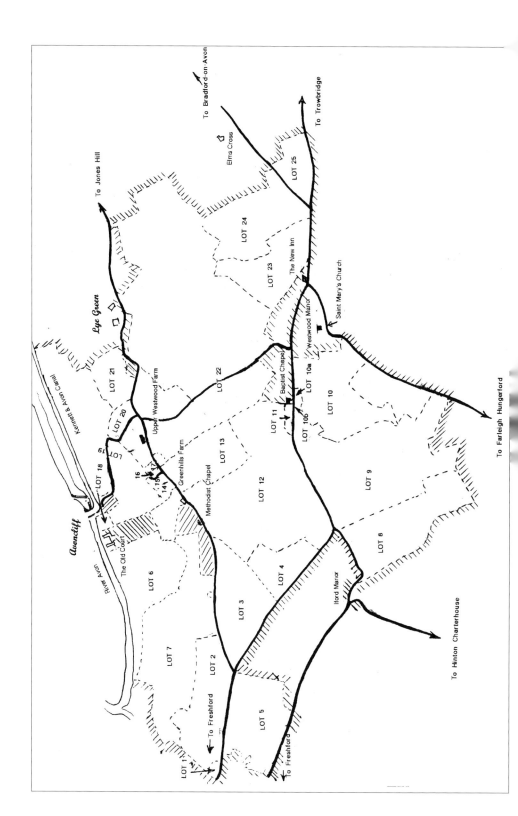

9	Building or Accommodation Land	14/05/1869	Fields to the south of Lower Westwood between Iford Lane and The Old School	Let to Mr John Marsh Still in agricultural use today
10	Exceptionally Rich Grazing Land	14/05/1869	Land to the south of Haygrove Farm and the Cemetery	Let to Mr John Marsh No houses here until 2000
10a	Piece of Freehold Garden Ground	Indenture of Conveyance from the Ecclesiastical Commissioners of the Church of England	The Old School Site	Powerful stuff
10b	Piece of Freehold Building Land	14/05/1869	Present site of Haygrove Farmhouse	Let to Mrs Hobbs and Mr Geo. Manners
11	Freehold Piece of Garden Ground	23/02/1867	Site of houses opposite The Old School	Let to Mr S E Marsh. Sub-let to Messrs Windo
12	Valuable Freehold Dairy Farm, Greenhill Farm (61 acres)	23/02/1867 & 14/05/1869	Greenhill House, garden and pasture, Friary Close, Great Orchard, Chestnut Grove, Westwood Park, The Pastures, Bobbin Park, Leslie Rise, Lister Grove, Boswell Road, The Croft, Farleigh View, Hebden Road, Tynings Way, Westwood Social Club	Parts let to Mr S E Marsh Sold for £1,500
13	Valuable Freehold Accommodation Land	23/02/1867	Westwood Park	Let to Mr SE Marsh No houses today
14	Pair of Old-Fashioned Attractive Cottages	23/02/1867	Probably 124 & 125 Upper Westwood and land on which 123 now stands	One let to Emily and William Hillier, the other to 'Keats'
15	Pair of large Modern Stone and Tiled Cottages	23/02/1867	Probably 115 & 116 Upper Westwood with land of the quarry yard	Let to Mr Rowland Hillier and Miss S Marsh
16	Pair of Modern Stone & Tiled Cottages	23/02/1867	Probably 113 & 114 Upper Westwood	Let to Messrs. Treman & Jones
17	Pair of Stone & Thatched Cottages	23/02/1867	152 & 153 Upper Westwood with grounds where 111 and 112 now stand	Let to Mrs Rains and Mr T Rains
18	Valuable Piece of Garden Ground	23/02/1867	Avon Villa, Avoncliff	Let to Mr S E Marsh

Opposite: Map showing the Lots to be sold at Auction

51

19	A Valuable Freehold Property	14/02/1869 23/02/1867 29/09/1873 & 30/09/1901 The substantial remainder a Statutory Declaration	Becky Addy Wood Quarry Wood, fields between the quarry and Little Court, the tramway, The Tump, sites of 117, 118, 119, 119A, 120, 121 and 122 Upper Westwood	Parts described as "pasture" let to Mr S E Marsh but quarrying licences for Bath Stone and Paving Stones remain with the previous holders
20	A choice little Freehold Property	14/05/1869 & 23/02/1867	Plum Cottage	Let to Edward Mallinson Esq. The lands let to Mr S E Marsh No more buildings
21	A Valuable Piece of Accommodation Land	14/05/1869	Fields to the north of Cottles Stables	Still agricultural use
22	Upper Westwood Farm	14/05/1869 & 23/02/1867	The farm, fields south to Linden Crescent and east to Lye Green	Sold for £3,000 Parts leased to Mr S E Marsh and to Mr John Marsh Still in agricultural use
23	A Valuable Piece of Accommodation Land	14/05/1869	The field behind the New Inn	Let to Mr John Marsh Still agricultural
24	Accommodation or Building Land	14/05/1869	The fields south of Elms Cross House	Let to Mr John Marsh Still agricultural
25	Valuable Freehold Building Site	14/05/1869	The field north-east of the road junction to Elms Cross	Let to Mr John Marsh Still agricultural

Sources

Victoria History of the Counties of England, Wiltshire Volume 7
The Westwood Manor Estates Sale Catalogue of 12 July 1911
The Church of St. Mary the Virgin, Westwood Guidebook by Simon Guy & Muriel Walker
Westwood Manor Guidebook by Denys Sutton

Mike Hawke

Childhood Memories of living at Westwood Manor

WHEN MR. E.G. LISTER bought the Manor House from Mr. Tugwell in 1911 it was nothing like the house we see today. It had been used as a farm since 1833 and was shabby, neglected and run down. He undertook to restore it with great sensitivity and the valuable and rare musical instruments which are on display were his own private collection. As well as being a proficient musician he also had a passion for needlework and many of the chairs in the Manor are covered with his fine work.

Westwood Manor, South and East Wings before restoration, 1912
(By kind permission of The National Trust).

His butler, Christo Moscoff, married one of the staff from Greenhill House in Upper Westwood and between them they more or less ran the house for Mr Lister. Their daughter, Diana Polhill, remembers being brought up there and writes:

"Mr Lister was a rather aloof figure. I doubt if he spoke to many of the villagers. He walked around with downcast eyes and his hands behind his back, deep in thought. He owned Manor Farm and the row of Manor Cottages opposite the New Inn and if any of the tenants had a problem they would come to my father and he would act as go-between."

Although one of Mr Lister's dislikes (and he had many) was children, he was quite tolerant of the young Diana, even giving her a Teddy Bear when she was two years old which she treasures to this day.

"He was a late riser, around midday, and went to bed at one or two in the morning. Just before retiring he would play the harp. He was not very accomplished, with a limited repertoire, so each night I was lulled to sleep by the sound of The Londonderry Air."

There were seven harps in the Manor at that time as well as a Bechstein grand piano which Mr Lister left to Diana in one of his Wills. (Sadly, his Wills were changed so often and used as a weapon and his final Will omitted that particular bequest. Things often used to get tense between the boss and his butler and when it became too fraught Mr Moscoff would threaten to resign, at which point, Mr Lister, realising he had gone too far, would leave a copy of his current Will in a prominent place!) There were also a harpsichord, a spinet and a virginal in the house, which are there today. Well known musicians came to visit Mr. Lister to make music and the Moscoff family enjoyed being invited to listen. The guitarist, Julian Bream and the harpist, Osian Ellis, are two names Diana remembers as well as regular visits from the clavichord builder, Mr Tom Goff.

Of his skills with a needle, Diana recalls:

"My memory of warm days is of seeing a large tapestry frame set up in the front porch with Mr Lister working away on the covering or cushion of a chair in an attractive Florentine pattern. I would sometimes accompany my mother when she was cleaning the linen press room where the cupboard enthralled me, as it was full of hanks and skeins of beautiful tapestry and knitting wool. Mr Lister was also a great knitter; mostly socks I seem to remember. But he did once knit me a jumper! I'm afraid I wasn't too impressed at the time as it was made from his collection of wools in stripes of sombre hue and I preferred jollier colours at that age!"

There were staff in the gardens of the Manor and Diana remembers:

"Before the Second World War the gardens were wonderfully tended. There were fruits and vegetables of every description. Neat beds were separated by stone paths edged with stone tiles. A wide herbaceous border ran the length of the garden from the pond gardens right up beyond the fruit cage and the tennis court to a high bank beyond which was yet another vegetable garden which over the years gave way to chestnut trees. A fruit cage was filled with soft fruits and there was a big strawberry bed. The length of the herbaceous border was lined with espaliered apple trees. There were two mulberry trees, gnarled medlar trees, quinces, figs, peaches, apricots and nectarines. A huge orchard with a great collection of cider apple trees bordered the road. Each autumn we would gather in the cider apples, banging them out of the trees. They were carted to the barn, minced up in a special machine and shovelled into the press between old blankets. Men from the village would come to man the presses, leaning on the great bars which turned the screw and pressed out the juice which was then pumped into great barrels in the lower barn. Anyone who asked would be given a jar of cider - which was an acquired taste! Eventually the cider apples were sold to Coates' Cider Company."

Christo Moscoff collapsed and died in 1954 at the age of 62. He had been trying to prepare the house for Mr Lister's return from his cottage in Devon. He had an appointment with a specialist, not having been well, but Mr Lister would not delay his return, thus making his butler cancel the appointment in order to finish the spring-cleaning of both house and garden. Despite feeling very bitter about her husband's death, Mrs Moscoff stayed on as cook for a further two years until she too was pushed too hard by her employer.

"My mother had prepared his dinner whilst he was on a visit to Bath. He returned bearing sprats and announced that he wanted them for dinner. My mother explained that she had already cooked dinner. Like a small child he said he didn't care. He wanted sprats. Mummy

Left: Christo Moscoff, the butler at Westwood Manor, 1919

Below: Westwood men returned from the First World War.
Left to right, front row: Joyce; Cottle; E. Jones; G Moore; Hube White; Bill Russell;
Second row: Roland Hillier; Bill Rogers; Jim Harris; Maslin; Ern Marchant; Len Windo; Bill Gane; Harry Cottle; George Cantello.
Third row: Shepard; George Poulsom; Frank Hobbs; Jimmy Raines; Ted Hobbs; Pop Harris; Reg Hobbs; Alb. Shepard; (unknown); George Hobbs.
Fourth row: Fred Mumford; Charlie Moore; Alb. Poulsom: Leonard Hobbs; George Mumford;
(unknown); Bill Moore; Horace Ostler; Gentleman George Hobbs. Back Row; Bill Mumford; Perce Moore; (unknown); Mr Ball; Fred Truman.

refused to cook them and he was furious. He was faced with giving in or dismissing her and he wouldn't give in! This time there was no Christo to sort things out so, despite entreaties from Mr Lister's friends, Mummy left."

Even so, when Mr Lister was killed in a car accident in 1956, he bequeathed to Mrs Moscoff several pieces of furniture and his beloved Old English Sheepdog, Gelert.

During 45 years of service to the Manor between them they had watched it being transformed from a nearly derelict house to a grand home visited by many dignitaries from all walks of life, and the Emperor of Abyssinia (Ethiopia), Haile Selassie and Queen Mary. (The pen she used to sign her name was kept in a glass case.) During the war, the Servants' Hall was commandeered to pile high with huge tins of food "against a blockade or invasion" and the Barn was used to store waste paper, another war effort, which was collected by the children in a hand cart. There was no gas or electricity (the latter was installed in 1953) which made the cooking quite a challenge on oil stoves and all the garden staff had been called up and some help was gained from prisoners of war. Life may have been hard for her parents but Diana feels privileged to have spent the first 21 years of her life at Westwood Manor.

Westwood Manor after restoration.

Westwood Manor Today

AFTER THE DEATH OF MR. LISTER in 1956, the Manor was left to the National Trust, as was specified in Lister's will. Denys Sutton, editor of Apollo Magazine, lived here as the first tenant of the Trust, then Katie and John Christophers moved here from St. Catherine's Court in Batheaston. They did some fairly extensive alterations to the old Servants' quarters, making the large sitting/dining/cooking room round which life revolves now. They enlisted the help and advice of Oswald Brakespeare, a distinguished architect, who used to arrive on a rickety bicycle, all the way from Corsham, looking immaculate, wearing his cycle clips. I have been told that he only had one leg - which makes the bicycle journey even more impressive! One of the things that we regularly bless the Christophers for was their decision to enlarge the kitchen and install an Aga; the only form of heating when we arrived.

In 1990, we were living in a tiny house (at least, now it seems so) in Shepherd's Bush in London with two daughters aged nearly two and four. I knew the area round Bath as my parents live at Midford, but we weren't intending to move down here at all. Then, on Easter Day 1990, my father brought us here and casually mentioned that the Trust was looking for a tenant. Equally casually, we rang the Trust the next day, said we'd love to take it and thought no more about it.

Some weeks later, to our great surprise, we were asked to come for "a preliminary interview." After this there was another long silence, but this time we couldn't forget about it because by then we had both taken the very risky step of setting our heart on the house and I had given in my notice at the school in London where I was teaching and applied for a job to teach at St. Laurence. My husband was frantically job-hunting down here and it all seemed very precarious and highly nerve-wracking.

On the morning of the second interview, I heard that I'd got the job, so I suppose the Trust realized that we were serious but the question that definitely clinched it was when they asked us what we would do with our own furniture if we lived here. We looked at each other for a moment and said that we were sorry but in fact we hadn't got any. Their faces lit up and from that moment onwards things went much more smoothly. I hadn't realised that they wanted the house to remain exactly as Lister left it and they really didn't want us to put anything of our own into the rooms open to the public, which included the sitting-room and our bedroom. (Of course, you don't sleep in a room every night for ten years without leaving some trace of modern life: Some years ago Class 3, Mr. Barker's class from Westwood School, came round and were set the task of drawing all the clocks in the house. Among the finished sketches was a detailed drawing of my husband's digital alarm clock.) Some people might not like that but it suits us as we like the house and its furniture just as it is.

Many people gave us dire warnings before we finally moved here in August 1990. The children would fall into the ponds; the stairs were far too steep and the children would have horrible accidents; there was no heating; we'd never find anyone to clean the house; we'd miss London; my husband would never get a job and the locals were a funny lot...And as for the idea, some years later, that this would be a suitable place for a poor little new baby!

None of these warnings was borne out and the locals couldn't have been nicer. Whether our children have been permanently damaged by growing up here I can't say but I very much doubt it. Though they do have a tendency to tell increasingly blood-curdling and totally untrue ghost stories to visitors.....

People who visit the house often mention its atmosphere of settled domesticity. Perhaps this isn't surprising when you consider that Westwood Manor is first mentioned in the year 983. In the Domesday Book, the house, which was much smaller - possibly even two separate cottages - is referred to as belonging to the Bishop of Winchester. By the thirteenth century, the monks had leased the estate out to tenants. By the end of the fifteenth century, the Culverhouse family were the tenants and Thomas Culverhouse must be considered as the virtual founder of the present Manor house. In 1480 he undertook extensive building work here, including the re-roofing of the main (east) wing. In the sixteenth century, the Horton family lived here and Thomas Horton connected the two halves of the house together by building the middle section containing the Dining Room and the Panelled Bedroom. The next phase of the Manor's development came in the seventeenth century, when the Farewells made it much grander by adding the porch, the turret and the stairs, creating the Music Room, and the elaborate plasterwork, including the curious double-tailed mermaid in the King's Room.

From the end of the seventeenth century and through the eighteenth, the house seems to have declined, though always lived in by tenant farmers. The Tugwell family of Bath leased it from 1775 until 1861, when the Dean and Chapter of Winchester sold the estate to them, and their descendants lived here until 1911 when Lister bought the house.

Of course there are eccentricities in a house like this. I am frequently driven to despair by the fact that the heating is designed to come on in warm, damp weather (think English summer) and go off when it's dry and cold (i.e. every time there's a frost). We appear to have more than our fair share of assorted household pests living with us (but we thank God for Mrs Rowe who wields her green fluffy duster menacingly at spiders, woodlice, ants and larger creatures, including the children). It isn't everyone's cup of tea to have their bedroom on general view and I have developed into the fastest bed-maker in the West after many occasions when I suddenly realize that the first visitors of the afternoon are on their way upstairs and I've forgotten to make the bed. Having the house open to the public three afternoons a week would be tricky if it weren't for an extraordinarily loyal and charming small band of House Stewards who help us.

But the eccentricities are what make the house interesting. Lister himself was clearly deeply eccentric. I love the stories about his terrible harp playing (apparently he used to blaspheme so colourfully when the strings broke that children would come and sit under the windows to listen) and his insistence that all visitors should stay up, freezing cold, till 3.00 a.m. doing yet more needlework by gas lamps. I like the way that every time I open a drawer I find more half-finished socks, knitted out of peculiarly lumpy and prickly-looking grey wool. None of that means to say that he wasn't a true aesthete and connoisseur when it came to how he restored the Manor. In the years when the National Trust was telling everyone to slap on a bit of acrylic paint over damp patches, Lister knew that Distemper and Limewash are the only paints which will stay on damp walls. He was way ahead of the rest when it came to conservation and painstaking research about the authentic materials to be used in plasterwork mouldings. Not that he wasn't keen to create his own highly idiosyncratic additions too. The front gate, with its huge off-centre sundial on top, gets odder the more you look at it.

Nothing detracts from the feeling of settled peace that comes from a house which has been here for so long. I love the feeling that nothing too eventful (at least, not historically eventful) has happened here; families must have lived through the usual births and deaths, squabbles, turmoils, big gatherings and quiet suppers here for far longer than in most places. I don't forget the feeling of repose which meets me every time I come up the steps to the house. I know everyone tells me that Lister was a thoroughly difficult and grumpy old toad who hated children and would turn in his grave to see life here now but then he was only one of a long line of people who have loved this house. I'm happy to think that we're in that line too, now.

Emily Azis

The Tithe Barn at Westwood Manor, West elevation, before restoration, 1912. (By kind permission of the National Trust).

The South Gable of the Tithe Barn at Westwood Manor has a crescent-shaped stone finial. The story about the finial is that on the under part or inside of the crescent are slight projections which, with a little imagination, could be said to represent a rudimentary form of insect legs. The legend goes that at one time in the Middle Ages the village was visited by "a plague" and some monks came up from Bradford and carved a stone locust and prayed round it till the plague had passed; the locust was erected where it now stands as a thank offering and a reminder to all and sundry who should pass beneath it on their way to church of the peril from which the village had once been delivered.

On the other hand, the crescent is thought to be a representation of the Goddess Ceres, she of the harvest moon. So you believe what you will.

Iford Manor

IFORD MANOR LIES in the unspoiled valley of the River Frome which runs down from the Mendip Hills to join the Wiltshire Avon a mile away at Freshford. Mentioned in a Saxon charter of the tenth century, the settlement at Iford owes its existence to the force of the river, which enabled an efficient water mill to flourish for the processing of cloth.

The first recorded occupant was William of Iford and his brother Nicholas in the early fourteenth century, who left property (which probably included the Mill and its large meadow) to the monks of Hinton Charterhouse. The monks held Iford until the Dissolution, but rented it first to John Horton, a clothier from Lullington in Somerset.

From 1543 until 1686 Iford remained in the possession of the Horton family who operated the Mill and extended the clothworking operations. Their dwelling was the part of the present Manor house facing the garden, which dates partly from the 1300's, while the side nearest to the yard was a separate building for stretching and baling cloth. (These parts of the building were joined up, possibly in the early seventeenth century, to create one house.)

Business was good. Thomas Horton, grandson of John, purchased more land and other mills for the manufacture of woollen cloth, such as the one at nearby Avoncliff, and he extended the buildings at Iford. He dedicated the Chantry in the church at Bradford-on-Avon and paid for the building of the church tower at Westwood. He lived at Horton House in Bradford, close to the Saxon Church. By the time he died in 1530, he also rented lands at Westwood and perhaps Westwood Manor itself (which was some three times larger than the part that remains today).

The next Thomas Horton, his nephew, purchased Iford at the Dissolution of the monasteries and it remained in the family until it was sold to the Hungerfords of Farleigh Hungerford in 1623.

At the end of the seventeenth century, the Mill had been let as a separate unit. After the dispersal of the Hungerford estate in 1686, Iford was sold to Henry Chandler, a successful salter from Bradford-on-Avon. During their tenure, at the beginning of the eighteenth century, the Chandlers re-modelled the front of the house in the classical style, with a five window central block flanked by small wings. The house changed hands several times through the Dingleys and the Hallidays after Eleanor Chandler's death in 1743.

Iford Manor with Britannia Bridge in foreground. (Tony Hawtin)

The Garden

In 1777, Iford was sold to John Gaisford, whose family had had connections with the wool trade in earlier times. Gaisford remodelled the garden and laid out the Great Terrace as a grass walk. He planted the hanging wood above the garden, and a number of the trees from that time can still be seen - woodland yew trees, box, beech, laurel and in particular, the large cedar tree above the hillside beyond the orchard and the great plane tree above the Great Terrace.

The Conservatory was built at this time, replacing a Chapel. Collinson's History of Somerset of 1799 mentions the previous existence of a Chapel and a Cloister and that the Chapel had been turned into a 'greenhouse'. There is no mention of it in the Parish records so it seems that it may have been a private, and possibly Catholic, Chapel, probably built and served by the Carthusian monks during their ownership of the property.

There were fine woodland walks above the garden with classical views. Several alterations were made to the interior of the house - among them the addition of a new stairwell and staircase and the creation of the Great Parlour out of the old staircase and two small rooms. Gaisford's son, Thomas Gaisford, was a churchman and distinguished classical scholar who, in later life, became Dean of Christchurch, Oxford. He continued the embellishment of the garden and grounds at Iford. In fine weather he would compose his sermons while walking up and down the grassy Great Terrace, but in bad weather he used the room to the left of the front door which is still known as the Dean's Parlour.

His son, another Thomas Gaisford, had the temerity to become a Roman Catholic, which caused such outrage among the local gentry that he decided to go elsewhere and sold the house to William Rooke in 1858.

The house became known for its house parties, with many guests coming from Bath to enjoy the fishing, to go by boat to the castle ruins at Farleigh Hungerford, or to take tea in the model dairy buildings of Dogkennel Farm across the river. After the death of Mrs. Rooke, Iford was bought in 1899 for Harold Peto by his sister, Sarah Crossley and subsequently purchased by Peto from her in 1903. By the time he moved to the area, the house and garden were in a neglected state.

Peto had been seeking his ideal country house for many years and immediately saw the possibilities of the place, although the task of restoring it was a daunting one. His alterations to the garden were commenced at the same time as his work on the house itself. Within the house he discovered that many parts of it were older than he had thought and undertook extensive and painstaking improvements and restorations.

Meanwhile, in the garden, he introduced several Gothic carvings of wood and stone to enhance the feeling of age and, by the time of his death in 1933, this man, who had created many great gardens in Britain, Ireland and the South of France, felt he had created his masterpiece at Iford.

Harold Peto's nephew, Sir Michael Peto, took on the maintenance of the property after his uncle's death. He and his family had the daunting task of trying to keep the place going in the period after World War II. The buildings and the garden, like so many other similar places, had suffered five years of wartime neglect and good materials and appropriate skills were in short supply.

The gardens were opened after the war on 31 March 1956 and the admission charge was one old penny (1d.)

By 1964 the Peto's decided to leave and Iford was sold to the present owner, Elizabeth Cartwright-Hignett. By this time, severe structural problems had become apparent in both house and garden buildings, due to the unstable geology of the hillside.

Much of Harold Peto's planting was over-large and due for renewal and there was an urgent need to undertake major works to ensure the survival of the architectural features in the garden, many of which had inadequate foundations. Some thirty-five years later, the owners are still trying to keep up with the tendency of places as ancient as Iford to crumble during any lapse in concentration!

There is an Iford Festival in the grounds every summer with music ranging from opera in the Cloisters to jazz in a fête champêtre setting. Visitors are encouraged to bring picnics to consume before concerts and small groups seated on rugs, sipping champagne and eating in anticipation of a good evening's entertainment, often accompanied by the delicate screaming of the local population of bats would surely meet with the approval of the long line of occupants through the years.

The gardens of Iford Manor are open to the public and visited by people who come from far and wide to enjoy the peaceful setting and, in 1998, "The Peto Garden at Iford Manor" won the Historic Houses Association/ Christie's Garden of the Year Award.

Old Mr Windo kept a white cow, which he used to drive along the road, grazing the verges on a summer's evening. ArthurPadfield was returning from a night out in Trowbridge, seated pillion on a friend's motorbike, when he noticed a white smudge ahead in the dimpsey and he shouted, "Look out - it's Mr Windo and his white cow", but before the words were out of his mouth they had hit Mr Windo and the pails on his yoke were spinning round and round. The naughty lads were laughing so hard that they did not stop and they almost drove into the river at Iford such was their mirth. But when Arthur's father was told what had happened the following morning, he was not amused and sent the boys to apologise and see if Mr Windo was all right. Luckily, he was fine and bore the boys no grudge.

From the Tump to the Manor
and back again

ETHEL FARMER, NÉE CANTELLO, was born in one of the cottages opposite the New Inn in 1919. The house was a tied cottage as her father was working at that time as a gardener at Westwood Manor. He worked in the gardens of several large houses in the district, including The Hall on Staples Hill, which was then the property of Mr Bythesea. Mr Bythesea left money for children who were regular attenders of the Wesleyan Sunday School. Mr Lister, of the Manor, held a Christmas party for the village children each year, where there was a huge Christmas tree with presents on it for each child. This was the highlight of the year and, after a lovely tea they were given, to take home, an orange, an apple and a bag of sweets. Another stage in her father's working life was when he worked as gardener at Winsley Sanatorium (now Avon Park Care Village) on the other side of the valley. He used to walk to work every day, and twice a day at weekends, when sometimes he would take the children with him to help collect the chicken's eggs. By 1927 the family was living in one of the wooden bungalows which used to be along the Tump. There was no running water: Mother kept a butt of rain water, but drinking water had to be fetched and carried by the children from one of the standpipes at either end of the Tump. Ethel remembers her father sitting in the back kitchen making wreaths, which he did expertly, and the children would collect moss in the woods for him. He would also pluck chickens for people and his wife would dress them.

Ethel attended the village school in Lower Westwood and can recall her fellow pupils being spanked in front of the rest of the class. Discipline was quite strict and in those days a rap over the knuckles was commonplace and the parents' response was that you probably got no more than you deserved. When she was 11 or 12 she left the village school and finished her education at a school in Trowbridge. She remembers that when they went to Bath by train they had to purchase their train tickets at The Courts as there was no ticket office at Avoncliff.

Before she married, Ethel was in domestic service. She was a parlour-maid at Iford Manor with Lord and Lady Peto, where there were 9 staff in the house: governess, butler, lady's maid, footman, house parlourmaid, under parlourmaid, cook, kitchen maid and nurserymaid. The Peto's gave their staff memorable Christmas parties but, due to the "oddities" of the butler, neither Ethel nor several other staff members stayed long. She then worked for Mrs Bayntun at Midway Manor where she was very happy. Finally, she moved to Bradford-on-Avon to work for the Misses Bessie and Agnes Bevan who were very good employers and she stayed with them until she married in 1939.

And now, never having moved far away, Ethel is once more living at the Tump in a modern house complete with running water and the days of carrying the water from the standpipe seem as though they never were.

The gardeners at Westwood Manor; George Cantello is second from the left.

Church and Chapels

It was a Welshman, Dylan Thomas, who exhorted us 'to begin at the beginning' and it was a Frenchman, Voltaire, who, in a sardonic comment on both English religion and English cuisine, wrote 'Il y a en Angleterre soixante sectes religieuses différentes, et une seule sauce', (in England they have sixty different religious sects but only one sauce). So where do we start an account of the church and chapels in a West Country village which, in its time, has seen Catholics, Anglicans, Methodists, Baptists and probably other groups long forgotten?

Let us begin at the top of the hill. From about 1840 a devout farmer in Upper Westwood opened his house for prayer and preaching to a small gathering in the Methodist tradition. This developed into the creation of a Methodist chapel in Upper Westwood in 1862 and this building, despite the inevitable ups and downs, largely flourished as a place of worship for almost exactly a century. At this point, with diminishing support, services ceased and, like a number of such local chapels, it was sold off and the now empty chapel was used for storage purposes. However, in 1972 it became a spacious and pleasant private residence , known as Broadview. Inevitably, from some angles, the building still has, to a degree, the distinctive look of a nonconformist chapel. Perched above the steep Limpley Stoke valley, it had a panoramic setting that few Methodist chapels in the land can have matched.

As with the former Baptist Chapel in Lower Westwood, however, the Upper Westwood Chapel needs initially to be seen in its local context as part of a long, dynamic nonconformist tradition, devoted to church worship and sundry good works. Non-conformism seems to have flourished nationally in areas where the cloth-making industry thrived and this part of Wiltshire was no exception; indeed, in his influential book *Twenty Golden Candlesticks* (published 1890), the Southwick Pastor, W. Doel, asserted that the West Wiltshire region 'for centuries had been a stronghold of dissent'. To exemplify, the great John Wesley himself first visited Bradford-on-Avon in the summer of 1739, when he rode into the town from Bath, on

The Methodist Chapel, Upper Westwood, before conversion in 1972 to a private residence.

which occasion he preached to a thousand people in Bearfield. Over the next fifty years he visited Bradford, a town he came to like, despite a mixed reception early on, some twenty-six times, often preaching in the open air to audiences of several thousand; his brother Charles was a frequent preacher in the district too.

A particularly good rapport with local Quakers was established. In 1755 a Methodist innkeeper, Richard Pearce, bought the Maidenhead Inn in Bradford and demolished its malthouse to make way for a chapel on the site. Methodism's popularity was such that a new chapel was ultimately needed and a bigger one was opened on Coppice Hill in 1818. The Wesleys had set up the Bradford Circuit in 1780 which comprised over thirty places in Dorset, Somerset and Wiltshire, including the chapel attached to Turleigh House; Bradford continued as head of this circuit until 1884 and is now part of the Trowbridge and Bradford circuit.

In Freshford, moreover, John Wesley reputedly preached eight times, once having to make himself heard above the din of the neighbouring church bells organised by a hostile local gentleman. Typically, in Freshford, two Methodist chapels eventually evolved, the original and the later breakaway, more fundamentalist Primitive Methodist one. Southwick had an exceptionally strong nonconformist tradition. In Limpley Stoke a small place of Baptist worship opened in 1815 but was replaced by a bigger, more up to date chapel in the late nineteenth century. Even the relatively small community of Avoncliff possessed a chapel close to the Ancliff Square complex, though admittedly this was mainly associated with the then workhouse.

So the Westwood chapels stemmed from a long local tradition of at least a century; one imagines a few kindred spirits meeting initially in private homes and then the need for a chapel arising as the movement burgeoned. It is small wonder that one villager said that she recalled the Westwood of her younger days as being probably 'more chapel than church'. But many such chapels in relatively tiny, remote villages were sold off in the twentieth century as populations altered in social character and as transport increased general mobility, enabling interested people to make their way to bigger centres of worship like Bradford, Trowbridge and Melksham.

However, in its day the Upper Westwood chapel was a central part of community life and was capable of holding one hundred and fifty people. Some villagers can still visualise the pulpit at the far end of the spacious chapel with its ranks of pews; the adjacent single storey building was for Sunday School and other meetings.

Services each week depended on whether or not a local preacher was available. Lay preachers often helped out but every two months the area minister himself took the service and preached; villagers remember one of them arriving at Westwood in a notably noisy, bone-rattling old car. If no one could take the service (bearing in mind the quite large number of congregations that needed supervising in the district) people would sometimes attend the Baptist chapel in Lower Westwood opposite the old school. The norm was a morning and evening service each Sunday, though in the latter days of the Methodist chapel, from about 1950, there was sometimes an evening meeting only, lasting around one hour and with a typical congregation of ten to twelve people. The children's Sunday School, supervised by Mrs Robinson and others, was generally on a Sunday afternoon.

This Sunday School, for children roughly in the five to twelve age range, was a major element in the chapel's work. Their numbers were swelled by children from Redditch families who had been brought down during the Second World War to Westwood to help in the Enfield factory underground.

Every Christmas the village mothers would produce a delicious tea for them all. Each year, too, there was a big prize-giving day when anniversary songs were sung and prizes for attendance were issued to the fortunate regulars. Mr Bythesea of Staples Hill, for example, left money in his will to help fund such prizes. The system was that points were given for attendance and, at the end of the year, those who had earned a total of over eighty points were given five shillings, a significant sum in those days - virtue rewarded.

Harvest Thanksgiving was, predictably in an essentially rural community, always well attended. A liberal selection of locally grown fruit and vegetables was displayed in front of the pulpit. The bread in the shape of a sheaf of corn traditionally took the most important place higher up.

Later the following week was the auction and again this annual event was popular and crowded. Presumably, even on such festive occasions, alcohol was conspicuous by its absence; even today, the owner of this former chapel is, by the terms of his purchaser's contract, not allowed to sell any alcohol on the premises, a ban perhaps common to all houses which were once Methodist chapels. Does this account for the presence of the old off-licence and shop building (Ashlers) a mere twenty yards away?

For the summer fete the trestle tables, covered in white cotton cloths, were brought out and placed alongside the hedge in the field now occupied by the Friary Close bungalows. Winnie Edwards and her mother lived opposite the chapel and helped to raise funds by selling knitted tea-cosies, lavender bags and other items lovingly made by hand. Hand-painted jars radiated colour with such items as green lavender and pink bath crystals, all symbolising the patience of an earlier, less hurried age. Teas were prepared in the steamy kitchen to the rear of the chapel's Sunday School area; hot tea and piles of sandwiches were taken across the road to the fete's helpers. It all combined to produce a day of hard toil and great enthusiasm, a reflection, to those old enough to remember it, of everything that is best in the true village spirit.

THE BAPTISTS

The old Baptist chapel is unobtrusively situated, as already indicated, near the former Schoolhouse in the main street of Lower Westwood. It was officially opened in 1865 and was one of three so-called village stations (the other two being at Upper Studley and Yarnbrook) associated with the very active Baptist chapel at Back Street, Trowbridge, which was supposedly the largest of its kind in the West of England apart from those at Bristol and Plymouth.

In his book *Twenty Golden Candlesticks*, Doel, somewhat amusingly and with manifest dissenting bias, writes of how, in Westwood, 'for centuries the Episcopal Church alone was the only place of worship in the parish and great ignorance and darkness reigned. It was not a bright spot of fair creation. Numbers were from time to time convicted at Wiltshire Assizes and transported.' (On this evidence one wonders how many descendants of former Westwood miscreants are now walking the streets of Sydney and Melbourne). Anyway, it was from this kind of dissatisfaction with the status quo that both Westwood chapels evolved. As in Upper Westwood, the Baptist one was prefaced by a few friends meeting privately for devotions in village cottages, though in this case the group shared a common belief in baptism by immersion. Preachers came over from Trowbridge, services mainly taking place in a house belonging to the aptly named Mr Godwin. Numbers grew rapidly and thus, again, the need for a proper chapel arose. A Mr Foster offered some land for the purpose, money was collected, and within a few months the small chapel, claiming to hold about ninety people, was opened for worship with pews, pulpit and pedal organ. The speed with which the chapel was built and paid for, partly via the Baptist Building Loan Society, testifies to the zeal of this founding group. In 1871 a Baptist Sunday School was opened but once more numbers grew and the chapel itself proved eventually too cramped for the purpose. Funds were raised for a new schoolroom, therefore, in the early 1880's, the foundation stone of which was laid by the Member of Parliament, G.P. Fuller. Completed in 1885, the building was about twice the size of the chapel and could seat some two hundred children; a reading room and other offices were attached. On special occasions such as anniversaries and tea meetings, this larger building, rather than the chapel, was used for services.

Since the chapel was a village station, its congregation were members of Back Street Chapel, Trowbridge, and men from the Preacher's Society connected with this urban 'mother church' visited Westwood regularly to assist with services. Writing of the benevolent influence of these early Westwood Baptists, Doel claimed that 'a good number have from time to time been saved in the village and have been baptised. Morally, religiously and socially speaking, the village and its inhabitants bear a different name today to that of fifty years ago....long may this little "Hill of Zion" prosper.'

The Sunday School building was more broadly used as an infants' school from the end of the Second World War until the present village school was opened. It has now been converted into a sizeable private residence. The chapel, too, was sold off a few years after the War and has since been used for various purposes, including storage. For a time it was the studio of the sculptor, David Backhouse, an example of whose work can be seen in the fine bronze head of the present Marquis of Bath in a library at Longleat House.

WESTWOOD CHURCH - THEN AND NOW

The Church of St. Mary the Virgin, Westwood, before the 1892 Parish Room was built.

Visible for miles around and dominating the Westwood skyline is the impressive tower of the present parish church of St. Mary the Virgin, which for almost a third of the millennium year 2000 has unfortunately been swathed in scaffolding as masons have laboured to secure the stonework and attend to any unduly wrinkled gargoyles. The tower's architectural importance can be measured by a framed copy of an article about it at the rear of the nave; this article, which discusses the so-called Westwood Group of Wiltshire Church Towers, was written by C.A. Plaxton, Vicar of Southbroom, Devizes.

These towers, he says, can be compared in quality with some of their celebrated counterparts in neighbouring Somerset, the Westwood tower itself being the finest and most elaborate in this area. Probably all the towers in this quintet (the other four are at Yatton Keynell, West Kington, Nettleton and Southbroom) were built by the same band of masons and the stone used is oolite from north Wiltshire. Plaxton concludes by saying, 'It should be a matter of satisfaction to all lovers of Wiltshire churches that in the Westwood type they possess a group of towers of which they need by no means be ashamed'. Clearly, too, the effect of the church is greatly enhanced when it is viewed close up as part of a most beautiful, tranquil and very English stone ensemble of Church, Manor House and Tithe Barn.

On a sadder, more negative note, many of the church's records were lost when a strong box, containing details of such events as marriages, births, baptisms and deaths, was stolen from the chancel a few years ago. These registers are, unfortunately, irreplaceable, which is galling for visiting family history buffs looking for information. In addition, even earlier, in the nineteenth century, some of the leaves from the church registers vanished, reportedly used by a churchwarden to help light his pipe inside the church. To make matters even worse, the ancient plate belonging to the church is also lost, pawned years ago by a dishonest parish clerk who died without disclosing the pawnbroker's name.

Around 1300 the church at Westwood became part of the larger parish of Bradford-on-Avon which meant that for many years vicars of Bradford, including men like the well-known nineteenth century antiquarian, Canon Jones (discoverer of the Saxon Church), also acted as vicars of Westwood and were responsible for services there.

The Church in detail

It is not clear when the first church was built on the present site but the proximity of the much-used Bath stone at local quarries makes a very early date probable. The chancel shows the most patent evidence of pre-15th century work and may have been part of this earlier building; its simplest, oldest features are 13th or even 12th century. The nave was rebuilt in the middle of the 15th century. The chapel and tower were added about the first quarter of the 16th century, probably under the direction of the then tenant of Westwood Manor, Thomas Horton, who had made his fortune in the cloth trade.

All these three features - nave, chapel and tower - are handsome examples of the Perpendicular style of architecture. The upper section of the tower has elaborately decorated parapets and pinnacles, while below these are several gargoyles in the form of grotesque animals, some of which are now headless. The AD 2000 masons claim that no gargoyles will have to be destroyed this time during their repairs, which is fortunate, because these carved grotesques are major contributors to the church's external effect. In any event, it is notoriously difficult and expensive to replace gargoyles because this entails penetrating deep into the surrounding stonework.

A spiral staircase at the south-east corner gives the tower further character and leads to the ringing chamber and belfry above. Originally there were four bells, three of which were mediaeval; these three predated the tower. The fourth bell was cast in 1677 and all four were then recast in the 1880's. In the 1950's the bells were declared unsafe, with rusty fittings, a shaky mounting frame and disconcerting vibration and thus were not rung for the next twenty years. In 1979, however, they were recast once again and made

into a peal of six, meaning that seven hundred and twenty changes could now be rung. The cost to the village was about eight thousand pounds and the hard-pressed vicar, Simon Guy, commented in the local paper about the difficulty of finding both money and volunteer ringers.

One of the most impressive features of the church is the mediaeval stained glass in the central panel of the east window. It portrays the Incarnation of Christ, symbolised by lilies, and the Crucifixion –

Three of the bells of Westwood Church which were taken down to be recast in 1979, with the Reverend Simon Guy on the right. (Wiltshire Times).

an exceptionally rare combination. The lily symbolism is almost exclusively English and the Westwood window is thought to be one of only seven examples extant. The east window's side panels, depicting angels bearing shields, seem to be roughly of the same date, early 15th century, as most of the glass of the chancel's lancet windows. Scholars (for the east window is important enough to have been the subject of learned articles in periodicals) think it likely that all this glass was originally sited in the Lady Chapel. The rest of the church's windows contain, at most, fragmented glass only and are not of comparable interest.

The nave was probably rebuilt in the late 18th century, perhaps under the direction of the Cox family, commemorated in a monument in the south wall. The moulded ceiling also probably dates from that time, executed by craftsmen from Georgian Bath. At the rear the font is supposed to be from the early 13th century, though its richly carved oak cover is from the 16th. century. Designed to discourage sin, an unusual, even 'double take' feature on the wall above the font is the large carved winged demon, which is also probably 16th century. He is variously known as 'The Old Lad of Westwood', 'the Devil of Limpley Stoke' and 'the Westwood Imp'. The demon is shown gnashing his teeth in frustration at the sight of each child newly baptised into the Christian Church and below is a barely legible inscription reading 'Resist me and I will flee'.

In the mid-19th century Canon Jones supervised a further restoration of the church. The west gallery was removed, which previously had been used by the village band to provide music for services, and new pews were installed. The Jacobean pulpit is said to have come originally from Norton St. Philip; Canon Jones found it abandoned at Tellisford. However, the present pews are relatively modern, dating from the 1960's, and the present organ arrived in 1987.

Another especially lovely feature is the carved oak ceiling in the chapel; it has a delicacy not always associated with oak. The western half of this has suffered from plastering, roof leakage and woodworm and has been restored without the ornamental woodwork, but the eastern half remains intact. In the chapel, too, traces of old frescoes, inscriptions and paintwork can be seen, especially at the eastern altar end.

Monuments & Memorials
The tablets and monuments around the walls are of great variety and interest. Perhaps pride of place should go to those which list the 20th century war

dead from Westwood. Thirteen names are recorded from the First World War:

John Walter Deverell; Henry Harford; Stephen Hayes; Walter Hazell; Reginald Tom Moore; Walter Mumford; William Arthur Randall; Arthur Joseph Ricketts; John Albert Ricketts; Ernest William Sheppard; Herbert Edwin Sheppard; Henry Arthur White; Herbert Wilcox

The accompanying quotation is:

"Greater love hath no man than this, that a man lay down his life for his friends."

The Second World War roll of honour is much shorter:

Frederick George Farrant
Lionel Henry Harris
Albert Edward Jones
Albert Mark Roper

Here the equally familiar quotation is:

"At the going down of the sun and in the morning we will remember them".

Near the organ there is a plaque in memory of Norah Windo, who died in 1946 at the age of twenty, having, remarkably, already been organist at the church for eight years. Another tablet records similar devotion: Alice Farley (died 1955), 'a worshipper and caretaker in the church for over sixty years', and Robert Farley (died 1972) who was secretary of the PCC for thirty years and church caretaker for seventeen. A stone plaque at the rear of the nave commemorates the talented Edgar Lister (1873 - 1956), 'who restored the manor house and lived in it until his death'. Opposite this is a marble tablet, faded but beautiful, in memory of one of Lister's predecessors at Westwood Manor, John Farewell (died 1642), with a six-line poem which neatly puns on Farewell's name. At the western end of the chapel there is a mournful epitaph to a young boy, seen as 'an early trophy of Death's conquering power', despite his youthful virtue and the piety of his parents. The celebrated Peto family of Iford Manor is also remembered by plaques and their coat of arms in the chapel : Harold Peto (died 1933), Architect and Designer of Gardens, buried at Chedington Church, Dorset; then

Sir Michael Peto (died 1971), churchwarden and benefactor, who died only three weeks after the death of his wife, Frances. Lastly in the nave there is the elaborate 1789 tablet (with verse) to Richard Cox, erected by his widow Mary, who died six months later at the tender age of forty-

Incumbents Since 1900

Records show that there have been nine incumbents of Westwood Church during the last century :

William Ruscombe Wollen	(died-1902)
Thomas Charles Clark	(1902-1908)
George Henry Kirkham	(1908-1944)
John Lindon Hamlet	(1944-1947)
Arthur William Taylor	(1947-1968)
William Francis Edward Burnley	(1968-1974)
Simon Edward Waldron Guy	(1975-1981)
Robert Alfred Loveless	(1982-1987)
Ronald Malcolm Lowrie	(1988-present)

In 1983 Westwood became part of the newly created benefice of Westwood and Wingfield that still exists today.

The present Rectory was built in 1964 for the Reverend Taylor in the garden of the Old Vicarage. Interestingly, it was built by Knee's of Trowbridge, one of the last houses they put up. The 1892 Parish Room beside the church has developed into a lively social centre for sundry meetings and exhibitions - and gossip over a cup of coffee!

GHOSTS & OTHER STORIES

Two ghosts are associated with the church. A path nearby is now known as 'Cabbots', believed to derive from 'Abbots'; here the figure of a monk is said to be glimpsed occasionally. A second phantom, a soldier in mediaeval dress, is said to appear sometimes to hurl a spear at the west door - perhaps a herald of Cromwell's iconoclasts?

Apart from these ghostly tales, anecdotes about the church seem few. I am indebted to Jean Warner of Chestnut Grove for the following atmospheric stories, however, and will quote her verbatim:

'At the christening of one of our daughters, the Vicar arrived in the church and couldn't find his glasses. He asked if anyone had seen them and everybody had a hunt round but couldn't find them so he said, "Never mind, I'll manage with this big book". So he tried but couldn't manage and asked one of the congregation to go and look in the Vicarage. Off she went and he went somewhere else, leaving the christening party waiting for what turned out to be half an hour before he returned triumphant with his glasses and the service proceeded'.

That was the Reverend Taylor. Mrs Taylor used to play the organ, which was then situated between the Lady Chapel and the main nave, and there were two seats either side of her which she tried to make Jean and Betty Hancock sit in so that she could hear them singing. They always refused as they felt embarrassed. However, when Mrs Taylor died, at her funeral service the church was full and the only two vacant seats were the ones she had always wanted them to sit in. They found that quite uncanny. The whole congregation then went in crocodile along Farleigh Lane for the scattering of Mrs Taylor's ashes. For quite some time after that, Jean avoided walking along there, especially when it was windy!

Another Vicar of Westwood, Simon Guy, a charming man, called on the Warners when Jean was in bed with 'flu. Jean had heard him arrive and when he left, Jean asked her husband, Dave, what he had wanted. "I don't know", said Dave. "He came in, sat down, picked up the paper and read it right through, put it down and said, 'I'm glad everything's going on all right', and left." He had been there about an hour and they never did discover why he had come!

The Future
The National Association of Decorative and Fine Arts Societies (NADFAS) has groups of volunteers who do Church Recording around the country. The Bath DFAS has this year completed the recording of Westwood Church and will present the bound book to the Parish at a Family Service in October 2000. They take a detailed inventory of everything in a church, including fixtures, movable ornaments, glass and so on. They research the history of each item through written sources and they then describe it in detail, with measurements and, if important, photographs. If an item is silver it is

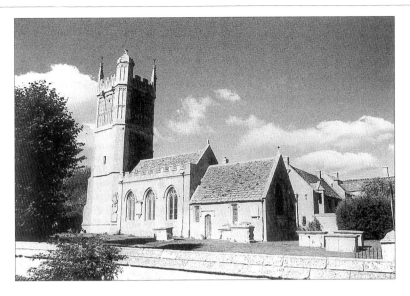

Church of St. Mary the Virgin, Westwood, with the Manor buildings behind. (S Snailum).

weighed and its provenance researched; the same applies to objects which have been donated. When the detailed recording is complete, the original bound copy is presented to the Parish; a copy of the original, with photographs, goes to the Council for the Care of Churches; a third goes to the National Monuments Record Centre in Swindon. A further three copies are presented to the Victoria and Albert Museum, the Diocese and the NADFAS library.

Let us hope that such records, lodged in safe places, will be there for future historians at the next Millennium.

John Holt

THE CHOIR'S REVENGE - quoted in an article about Westwood by Mrs Wheatcroft in the *Bath County Graphic*, December 1898. The following story was told by a Victorian cleric:

Whilst on the subject of Westwood, I perhaps may mention one olden custom that I think was probably unique. In 1851 our choir sat in a western gallery and was led by divers instruments, flute, fiddle, violin, cello and, on special occasion, we had a French horn or cornopean, and sometimes a trombone. The chief farmer, who was also churchwarden and had been active in introducing the new Poor Law system, was very unpopular. The villagers literally persecuted him; they stole his chickens, ham-strung some of his horses, and took a side of bacon from his kitchen and buried it in the churchyard.

He was at open war with them, and sent not a few ultimately to prison. He used to tell me with glee how many he had prosecuted. The revenge taken by the villagers was shown in church in certainly a singular way. They always sang a particular psalm - we used Tate and Brady - after anyone had been sent to prison. Standing in the middle of the gallery, Jasper Wheeler, the choirmaster, gave it out with the old formula of singing to the praise and glory of God, always looking down on the farmer, whose seat was below. The psalm was the 36th., the first verse of which ran thus:

> My crafty foe, with treacherous art,
> His cunning purpose would disguise;
> But reason whispers to my heart
> He sees no God before his eyes.

When I removed the west gallery, I found in it this writing: "On (date) Mr Sprackman sent George Hobbs to prison; next Sunday we sang the 36th. Psalm". This fully interpreted the custom to me.

The above article was printed in the *Westwood News* of October 1993.

In January 1994 another article about Westwood by Mrs L Wheatcroft in the *Bath & County Graphic*, December 1898 was produced in the *Westwood News* under the heading:

The Disappearing Vessels

The following story about Westwood was told by the Victorian cleric, Canon Jones:

My benefice included Westwood, though I never read myself in there. There was but one service each Sunday, held alternately morning and afternoon, in that church. The curacy had been held for nearly a quarter of a century by a very good, learned and eccentric man, the Rev. Martin Longmire. He was a good Hebrew scholar; so his Cambridge friends facetiously gave Longmire the sobriquet of

Talmud. He was one I reverenced much for the simplicity of his character and for his genuine piety. He became in his latter days very deaf and partially blind. A dishonest clerk pawned the Communion vessels, which he was wont to take out again on the day before Holy Communion was celebrated. At last, unable to pay the money for redeeming the said vessels, he persuaded Mr Longmire to alter the days of celebration - these were but three in the year - and borrow the Communion vessels from Winkfield. The old gentleman was not in the least aware of the deception. The sudden death of the clerk, who never fully disclosed his secret, prevented our ever discovering the pawnshop in which they were pledged and they were lost.

Mr Longmire himself supplied a plated set in their place, saying with all good humour as he gave them to me: "Many clergymen, after 25 years' service get a piece of plate presented to them; it has been my lot to have to give some plate to the Church".

I may mention, as a reminiscence of those days, that on one of my visits to Westwood, I found the churchwarden seated in a pew in the chancel smoking a pipe and reading a newspaper. I remonstrated; but all I got back was the remark that it was very hot weather and he found that a cool place.

On looking behind the Communion Table, I espied an old register, which I rescued and had bound. Some leaves were unfortunately missing, and so I strongly suspect that they had been torn out to light the 'churchwarden' which he smoked.

Margaret Boulting and "Jetty" outside their Red Bungalow in Tynings Way.

Westwood in the Second World War

Until the Second World War nothing much had disturbed the essentially rural life of Westwood; the two halves of the village continued to have their own existence except for activities such as going to church or the children going to school in which case it was necessary to make the trek from Upper to Lower Westwood.

The advent of the war really put the village on the map and the principal reason for this was the quarries. Being away from the large urban areas which were obvious bomb targets it was considered to be a much safer place in which to manufacture guns. And so The Royal Enfield Factory brought many of their staff from Redditch in the Midlands to Wiltshire.

Those who had lived here all their lives were in for no small culture shock as different groups of incomers moved in to the village. To provide accommodation for their workers, Enfield erected what amounted to a small village on the area now occupied by Bobbin Lane and the Council Estate, between Upper and Lower Westwood. Wimpey Construction employed southern Irish builders to put up what were known as the Red Bungalows for the Enfield workforce. These bungalows were supposed to be good for ten years but, in the event, they remained on the site for more like 30 years. The walls were but one brick thick and those brave enough to attempt wallpapering to try to make them more attractive were unable to achieve anything approaching a decent finish. Plain paper peeled off with the damp and showed every crack and hole in the surface - so, the only way to overcome these problems was to use paper depicting busy scenes of fox-hunting and rural views which disguised the unsightly bits that stuck out with a fox hole or a copse or a ploughed field! It was also inordinately cold in winter with icicles hanging inside. The roofs were made of corrugated asbestos and when it rained the noise was deafening. The foremen of Enfield were accommodated in slightly bigger houses where The Croft is now.

As well as the Red Bungalows there was a sick bay, a canteen, bachelor quarters and, the jewel in the crown, the Assembly Hall. This was where the Enfield workers could relax and play cards or billiards or other activities;

and there was a dance floor which became known as "the best in the West" and was the envy of people for miles around. Initially, this facility was strictly for the use of Enfield workers only, much to the indignation of the villagers, but later on they were able to use it and were also able to attend the ENSA concerts held there.

The Concert Hall inside the Enfield Assembly Hall. © Crown Copyright/MOD

Not only was there the workforce which came from the Redditch factory to Westwood; there were local people employed in the manufacture of gunsights for tanks, radar instruments and anti-aircraft guns. One man who came from Bristol said that his first impressions of Westwood were that it was, "a closed community and we were not welcome." The area of the Red Bungalows was known by the locals as "the site" and the two groups of village inhabitants did not mix with each other. Of course, the villagers had to continue to provide their own amusements, being unable to attend the events at the Assembly Hall at first, which must have added to the feeling of resentment of these "incomers" taking over the area.

Whilst the Irish labourers had been in the village constructing the Enfield site, they lived in wooden huts in a field in Upper Westwood at the top of the road down to Avoncliff; when they left, their accommodation was taken over by American soldiers in about 1942. It has been recorded that: "Their arrival was welcomed by the young women of the village, for these soldiers had money to show them a good time; they were also welcomed by the children with their endless supply of candy; but not so much by the men of the village who resented their wealth and intrusion. Many of these soldiers were black, which was a new experience for the local people who had only seen black men in films."

The American soldiers duly left and then came Polish refugees who stayed in the single men's hostels in Bobbin Park. The Poles were not only from foreign parts, but they spoke an impenetrable language which meant that there was very little mixing between them and the villagers. In any case, the refugees were mostly employed outside the village and tended, when here, to keep themselves to themselves.

One must not forget the evacuee children who came to the village to escape the Blitz in London. They were billeted in different homes around the village and had to attend the already crowded village school. One of them, Laurie Curness, recorded his impressions of life as an evacuee in Westwood from 1940-1945. He remembers leaving Paddington station with both arms in slings and the next thing he was standing with 89 other children waiting to be selected for a billet. But nobody wanted this little boy with two arms in slings and so he was last to be placed. However, he thinks he did very well out of it because he was placed at the Post Office in Lower Westwood with "Auntie" Bella Windo and her daughters, Molly and Gladys. After London it seemed very quiet but two weeks after he arrived he heard from his mother that their home had been flattened by a bomb.

He used to attend the Baptist Chapel by Orchard Close and sensed that the village was divided between "chapel" and "church". Every Saturday morning he would use Molly's bicycle to go into Bowyer's in Trowbridge to do the shopping for the cluster of people in that part of Westwood; the order was the same every week - 10 pounds of sausages and 7-8 caraway seed cakes! He took part in the paper collection for the war effort and every Thursday night there was great excitement as a Smith's Crisp van came to the New Inn - but they were only allowed two packets each. Also on Saturday, he used to go ferreting down at Iford to catch rabbits for the pot.

He remembers he had daily chores to do which comprised filling buckets with water from the pump and pumping water into the loft for baths as well as feeding and mucking out the chickens. He also used to help with the cider making in the barn at the Manor in the autumn and with haymaking, the harvest and charlock picking. By the time he returned home to London he had earned £15 in Savings Certificates.

He appears to have happy memories of his war in Westwood - particularly

"Auntie" Bella's banana spread, made with parsnips and banana essence (!) and the parties given at the Manor for the evacuees.

History does not relate whether the evacuees were allowed to attend the Royal Visit in 1943 of Queen Mary. She came to open the Assembly Hall and to visit the Red Bungalows as part of a morale boost for the workers.

The Home Guard operated from the wooden hut which later became the present day Social Club and, although no bombs fell directly on Westwood, some slight damage resulted from the vibrations emanating from the heavy bombing of Bath. There was, apparently, some strafing over the village as aircrews got rid of unused ammunition before returning to Germany and they let off several rounds in the direction of the Irish workers' wooden huts but no injuries were sustained apart from one slightly hurt Irish nose!

When Victory in Europe was declared in 1945 the whole country celebrated; but Upper and Lower Westwood had their separate street parties! In Lower Westwood people remember dragging a piano into the street for a good old al fresco singsong.

Guns and other artefacts of war no longer being required, Enfield continued to make use of the quarry and the "site" and provided employment for many of the village people when they turned to making motorcycles and motorcycle parts. And still there were "outsiders" coming to Westwood. Having been employed in the Radstock quarry and on local farms, Italian prisoners of war were located in the Enfield hostels whilst waiting to be repatriated. At that time, not surprisingly, one could sometimes enjoy a little opera singing on the local buses as these men brought a flavour of Italy to Wiltshire.

In 1950 the Enfield Cricket team was formed. Up until that time the village cricket team had played in various locations; the first was where the bungalows near the Social Club are; then there was one in Elm Hayes field up behind the New Inn on Bob Holdway's farm. It then moved to a different site within that same field and, subsequently, to the field next to 56 Lower Westwood. In dry summers the problem of keeping the pitch watered was resolved by forming a human chain with buckets filled from the well at the entrance to the village. So, never having had a proper permanent pitch or a pavilion, the Westwood cricket team was virtually taken over by the Enfield club, which set up a pitch where the current Westwood with Iford School is. At this time there was a slight thaw in the attitude towards the "site" and its occupants, many of whom stayed on and made the village their home when Enfield finally left.

The last influx of "outsiders" came with the arrival of Hungarian refugees fleeing Communism after the uprising of 1956. Once again the language barrier prevented any integration, though the Hungarians were probably the least popular of all the visitors Westwood had had and they were not here for long.

So the War had brought strangers to the village, brought industry to the village, doubled the density of housing and blurred the edges of Upper and Lower Westwood, making it one larger community instead of two separate neighbourhoods. There would be no going back to the quiet rural ways of the two small communities.

The development of the village in the post-war years has been researched by Christine Windo:

"In the late 50's the first building since the war commenced. Westwood's first council houses were built at Farleigh View and Hebden Road and marked the beginning of major construction within Westwood which got under way in earnest in the 60's. This development was to continue to the 80's and beyond, changing the small rural village of Westwood into a collection of large modern estates with parts of old Westwood dotted in between. The onset of war had initiated the development and now the pressure of a growing population began to be felt by the village - development which would change Westwood from a community to a dormitory village was about to begin.

Modern bungalows in Tynings Way replacing Red Bungalows.

"In 1966-7 the first houses on the "site" were demolished, to be replaced by new, modern council houses. While the new council houses were being built, the residents of the old Red Bungalows were shunted around in sequence from house to house until their house was ready for them to move into. Soon the last of the Red Bungalows was demolished and the whole character of that part of Westwood had been changed. As Enfield had moved away by then, this left the hostels and the Assembly Hall falling into disrepair; so they were demolished in the late 70's. Thus, it seems that not only had the coming of Enfield had major effects on the village, but the leaving of Enfield also. Now Westwood had lost its main centre of entertainment and from now on its newly found community spirit began to decline again.

"Further development commenced with the building of the first non-Council estate, Linden Crescent; a small modern estate of about 20 houses built on the field known as Pye Croft. The houses were designed to attract people in a higher income bracket who worked outside Westwood but wanted to live in the country - the first sign that it was going to become a picturesque dormitory village. This estate was quickly followed by "The Pastures", a much larger estate of houses, also designed to attract people in the higher income bracket."

"The Pastures" was built on fields known as Hibbards Ground, Warrensfield and Clay Piece. Other small cul-de-sacs, such as "Chestnut Grove", built on Little Fore Close in 1963, were developed and thus Westwood was quickly becoming a much larger modern community. The wooden huts in Upper Westwood built to house the Wimpey builders, were taken over by squatters until they were demolished in the 60's.

One of the last remaining Enfield contributions to the village finally disappeared in 1975-6 when the current Westwood with Iford Primary School was built on the site of the cricket pitch. Since then Westwood has been without a cricket team. The last of the Enfield dwellings was knocked down in 1999, having been condemned as it was constructed mainly of asbestos. On the plot where that bungalow stood at Windy Ridge, there are two "executive" homes under construction in the year 2000.

Susan Snailum

Thanks to Christine Windo for allowing me to use parts of her A-level project, "Westwood 1940's-1980's" for this article.

Two houses under construction at Windy Ridge, in 2000, on the site of the last Enfield Building. (S Snailum).

Working Underground during the War

LILY MEAD was conscripted, like all young people over 18 who did not have what were known as "key" jobs. They either had to go into the forces or work in factories. Lily was working in a cardboard box factory in Bristol at the time and was sent, with many others, to a retraining centre. There were shopgirls and office girls and girls who did not already have a job, most of whom had never seen inside a factory, let alone worked in one. It was a four month course learning to work on machines which made metal objects, mostly precision work. If you completed the four months you were then termed a 'skilled' worker but Lily only did two months there and was therefore classed as 'semi-skilled'.

She remembers arriving by train at Avoncliff with two others from the centre - they had had to travel in the end carriage so as not to miss the platform - and walking up through the woods to Westwood. It felt very strange to them and they had to report to a man in a wooden hut near the quarry before being taken to the hostel. This was when the Enfield works were only getting under way and the workers were all beginning to arrive. "Down Under" as the quarry was known, was also getting tooled up with a lot of the machinery coming from America on the lease-lend scheme. Lily's future husband had arrived from Redditch three months earlier and he was a "key" worker.

The situation underground was ideal; all the stone, ceilings and walls were whitewashed and there were heating ducts all around so that the temperature was stable all year round at about 65 degrees. This entailed a mass of electrical wiring and there were two electricians permanently working down there. There was a small tea bar at the entrance to the quarry where the workers had a quick cup of tea and there was a sun room, supervised by the resident quarry nurse, with two sun lamps on either side of a small underground room. Two people sat side by side facing in opposite directions, with bare torso and wearing tiny black goggles, to be exposed to the lamps' ultra-violet rays for no more than two minutes. This was felt to be a good thing in view of the fact that the workers were underground all day and every day and so rarely saw the real sun. The surgery also supplied all the workers with halibut oil.

Lily was employed making predictors, which were instrumental in spotting aircraft and all the different sections making different parts were separated from each other for security purposes.

She began in the grinding section and ended up on the lathe, having learnt a lot from her future husband, Charlie, who was foreman in the tool room making precision instruments. He was a patient teacher and all the young men and women he trained admired him and had a good word for him.

After a long day working underground from 8 a.m. until 7 p.m., including Saturdays, with only one weekend off a month, the workers needed their food. In the hostel, the food was very sparse to start with when there were not many staff, but after a few months, more staff arrived and the food improved enormously. The village people were very kind and gave extra rations to the workers, like eggs and chickens and home made jams - all things which were very hard to come by during the war. But Lily remembers that, on the whole, the Ministry made sure that their workers were well fed and they lived very well as the war progressed.

In the hostel, rooms were either single or double and there was a housekeeper in the women's hostel. They were supposed to be in at a certain time, but the windows were low enough for them to climb in after a night out! After a time they were moved from the wooden hostel to a more substantial brick one which was where Bobbin Lane is now.

It was not all work, however. Enfield looked after their staff and there were entertainments laid on at the Assembly Hall and dances with Eddy Purnell and his Band. Lily and Charlie used to go into Bradford-on-Avon Town Hall (now the Roman Catholic Church) to play Badminton. She remembers that, on the whole, people were happy and there was a very good atmosphere.

Lily gave up work to become a housewife when she married Charlie in 1952 and she was then able to visit her parents in Bristol more often and Charlie stayed on at Enfield's until they closed.

When the war ended in Europe, those who wanted to leave could do so but Enfield continued to run a large operation in Westwood, no longer making gun parts but motorcycles. These were assembled in the dance hall of the Assembly Hall, at which time Enfield's built a wooden hut as a replacement leisure facility for the village. As the Assembly Hall had been

The lounge in The Enfield Hostel. © Crown Copyright/MOD.

The Bar in The Enfield Hostel. © Crown Copyright/MOD.

A dance in the Assembly Hall with Eddie Purnell and his Band in the 1940's

officially a "temporary" structure and there were not the means to maintain it after the war, it was demolished along with so much else and the land where it stood is now a part of Bobbin Park, which lies near Windy Ridge between Upper and Lower Westwood.

When Lily went down the quarry recently, she was surprised to see that much of it seemed unchanged; the office where her husband worked was almost as she had last seen it. It brought back memories, though, of how alarming it used to be when there was a safety drill for the workers. They were working in the brightly lit, whitewashed and heated areas and when the alarm sounded they had to down tools and scuttle right through to the entrance at the other end of the Tump. The awful darkness, dampness and spiders of those normally unpenetrated parts of the quarry do not feature in her otherwise happy memories!

LUCY HARPER came to the village in February 1942, aged 28, with her husband and two small boys. Her husband had been working for Bristol Aeroplanes and was offered a transfer to the Enfield works at Westwood. They had been living in Thornbury, 17 miles outside Bristol, which was, at that time, a busy garrison town and a target for bombing raids. So a transfer to a quieter, perhaps less risky country village, was an attractive prospect. At first they were housed in one of the Red Bungalows, which was very cold, despite being allowed 2 cwt. of coal by the Ministry of Defence. But she says, "I thought I was in heaven here; you could get into bed and go to sleep."

Her two boys had to attend Westwood School and they were not happy there because, not only was it extremely crowded with the influx of Enfield children and evacuees, it was already a very old building in urgent need of improvement. After the age of 12 the boys moved on to school in Trowbridge.

Lucy and her husband worked underground. Her job was to build gyros used in firing the naval big guns and then she worked on underwater cameras. Not only was the work interesting, but it brought in extra money and gave her a purpose in a village where she did not know anyone. In later years, she and her husband sometimes discussed the possibility of leaving the district and moving on but the boys were settled and by then Westwood had become their home.

Interview by Kimberly Milne-Fowler

BETTY HANCOCK (née Orchard) remembers living in a red bungalow:

"I was born in Westwood in 1933, one of twins and the youngest of 9, in a small cottage opposite Linden Crescent. At the age of 3 months myself and the whole family, moved to Winsley.

I married in 1953 and, as my husband worked for the Enfield Cycle Company, we were allocated one of the Red Bungalows. This was quite exciting as I had never experienced a bathroom or indoor toilet.

The walls were built with single cavity bricks and the inside was not plastered. The roofs were asbestos. Consequently, it was hot in summer and cold in winter. Using Paraffin heaters in most rooms made a lot of condensation on the walls which, when very cold, turned to ice.

When decorating we always tried to get wallpaper that would disguise the bricks. The bungalow we lived in, in Haygrove, had 3 bedrooms, a fair sized living room, a small kitchen and a bathroom. The fire in the living room not only heated water, but an oven in the kitchen.

We had a large garden so were able to grow lots of vegetables.

We lived there for 13 years, moving to another bungalow in Hilborough Road whilst ours was demolished so that Boswell Road could be built. After a year we moved to Boswell Road in nearly the same position as we were in the Red Bungalows."

A Red Bungalow.

LIONEL SHEPHERD has lived in Westwood since 1963 and remembers his first home here, one of the Enfield bungalows, with fondness. They were easy to manage, cosy and made a lovely home. What's more, they were equipped with a cooker and a gas refrigerator. The rent was 10/- (50p) per week, plus 2/6 (12p) extra if you had a TV mast and aerial. When the Enfield works closed down, the houses were sold to the Council for £50 each. They were then demolished by "Eric" (who only had one tooth) who reckoned he got £150 for each one he disposed of. New Council homes were built in their place and Lionel moved in to his present home in 1967 for a weekly rent of 17/6 (87p).

Interview by Rodney Hutchen

DAVID & JEAN WARNER both came to Westwood because of Enfield's. David's father worked for them at Redditch and in 1941 moved to the munitions factory in the quarry at Westwood to be a capstan lathe operator on gunsights. Jean's father worked for Enfield's in Bradford-on-Avon but was allocated one of the Red Bungalows in Westwood. David emigrated to Australia with his parents under the £10 scheme but came back after four years.

After the war, Enfield changed its Westwood operation from making gun parts to making motorcycle engines until 1971. David had been a motor mechanic in Australia and when he returned to Westwood he got a job assembling the motorcycles. After a year, he was invited to be a tester for the 750 Interceptor machine, which he enjoyed enormously. Meanwhile, Jean was going to work in Trowbridge every day and, when she gave up her pushbike and invested in a moped, her travel times altered and it so happened that her journeys coincided with the motorcycle testers' runs. Jean and David married in 1963 and in that same year, Jean's mother, Mattie Barker, bought the Post Office in Lower Westwood from Mrs Gibson. She also bought the old Baptist Chapel opposite which she used for storage and had a little kitchenette and toilets installed. However, she was no businesswoman, being too kind hearted to make a profit; and when the new village Post Office Stores was built in Tyning Way, she moved there and ran

Interceptor Mk IIs outside the Quarry. On the left is hill-climb champion Chris Ludgate, with Plant Manager, Roger Shuttleworth standing and David Warner on the right. (From 'Best of British Bikes' by Jim Reynolds).

it until she retired in 1971.

In 1943 Queen Mary came to visit the Assembly Hall and the Red Bungalows and workers' names were put into a hat to decide whose bungalow the Queen would visit. She arrived in a very smart car and that was the first car that David had seen! (The first time he rode in a vehicle was when he and several other Westwood children were rushed to Trowbridge Hospital with scarlet fever).

When Enfield began their motorcycle operation, they used the Assembly Hall for assembling the machines and, having removed that facility from their workers, they built a new wooden hut for use as a social club, situated at the northern end of Bobbin Park opposite the large airshaft. David and Jean lived at Chestnut Grove by that time and when David drew back the surrounding cars and houses were covered in ash. When the police came to ask them what, if anything, they had heard during the night, they were totally baffled - they had heard nothing. The rest of Westwood, on the other hand, had had very little sleep due to the noise of bottles exploding and the commotion of the Fire Brigade arriving.

Matty Barker and Doll Coombes outside the Post Office in Lower Westwood in the 1960s

The Children's War

ALTHOUGH THERE WERE lots of changes in the village during the war, we children were for the most part spared most of its horrors. None of the fathers of my friends were "called up"; any bombs that dropped, fell harmlessly, except for the ones dropped on Trowbridge and, of course, Bath. It was the arrival of strangers to a close-knit community dominated by a few families which caused the biggest upheaval. The arrival of the evacuees was a big event. Suddenly, here were all these children from London who could have been from another planet. I remember them arriving in Lower Westwood, each clutching a carrier bag of possessions, waiting to be assigned to a family. Although we were not having anyone, my mother soon received an urgent summons from "Auntie" Molly Windo. She and her mother, "Auntie" Bella, had been given a BOY! Please would my mother come and bathe him! That was Laurence Curness, whose own memories appear in another chapter. He did not seem to suffer from his experiences and "Auntie" Molly was the most wonderful of people, especially to small children. Her house was second home for me and for many other children.

The biggest upheaval was the building of the "Site" in the fields between Upper and Lower Westwood, with the much lamented loss of the Cricket Field. It was built by Irish labour and each payday you could hear them carousing up the road after the pub closed. The "Site" was to house the Enfield Cycle Company employees, evacuated from Redditch to work in the factory built into the underground quarries. Apart from the houses, a splendid Assembly Hall was built, primarily for the use of the employees of Enfield's. There was a cinema show on a Sunday and dances were held there too. It was all so amazing and sophisticated to us children. There was even a twirling ball of mirrors twinkling over the dance floor. For the most part though, the Hut remained the venue for village activities. We children put on concerts of a very amateur nature but we always got a good audience. If we could not find a hall then we lured anyone prepared to pay tuppence into a field behind the New Inn and put on an entertainment. The grown-ups gave us an annual tea party and then dressed up and did skits on the latest things on the radio or cinema. We had fancy-dress competitions and it was amazing how ingenious people were, considering clothes were rationed. It was a wonderful non-materialistic time. Parents were not driven mad by demands for the latest toy or gimmick as there was so little to buy. If they could, they improvised. I had a lovely set of dolls-house furniture made from empty matchboxes. No one feared for what might befall you if you were out of sight in those days. We were given a packet of jam sandwiches and a bottle of lemonade and off we went to play in the fields or lanes, making "houses" or hairdressing the grass at the side of the road or walking to Iford to paddle in the river at Brockles. We had the freedom of each others' houses and we were all known by the old villagers, so always felt secure.

Each Friday evening, armed with 6d, those of us living in Lower Westwood would advance on the New Inn, tap on the side window to attract the attention of the publican's wife and ask for "A bottle of ginger beer and a packet of crisps, please"! We would then play around together.

Sometimes there was the excitement of an army jeep going by, but usually there was nothing to disturb our games of hopscotch chalked on the road with a bit of stone.

The highlight of the year was a visit to the pantomime in Bath. About eight of us would go, including "Auntie" Molly. We would go by train from Bradford, an adventure in itself. We girls would be enthralled by the costumes and a game we played was to say as each dress appeared, "Bags I that!" After the show we indulged in fish and chips. There was a bus service of sorts to Bath, which was quite an adventure, as the route was quite complicated, due in no small part to the fact that all signposts had been removed from the roadsides and the bus driver was continually being screamed at as he took a wrong turning!

For a while, there were soldiers billeted in the Parish Room. They had to come to the Manor to fetch water. One of them 'fell' for the maid, Olive, and they became engaged. She later regretted her rash promise when she joined the WRNS and met someone else and there was quite a to-do about 'breach of promise' before she became free again. The Parish Room was then used for less dramatic activities. You could collect wool to knit socks, balaclavas and scarves for the troops. Everyone with an aptitude knitted and you sat and listened to the radio whilst you knitted.

There was a wonderful sense of community. At haymaking time, the children all 'helped' and were rewarded with swigs of scrumpy cider. One of my proudest moments was being told by Mr Seward that I was the only child drinking out of the bottle the right way, with the rim pressed to my upper lip! We were tolerated in the farmyard and enjoyed watching the butter-making and the milking. Horses were still used for hauling and ploughing. They were still used by the baker, too, and the bread arrived in a horse-drawn van.

When the end of the war was announced on the radio, I ran down to the corner and excitedly announced, "The war's over!" "We know", was the chorus from people standing around their front doors. It was also the end of an era!

Diana Polhill (née Moscoff)

Wings for Victory Presentation, 1942.
Left to Right: Len Windo: Molly Windo: Glad Farley: Joe Foster: Bet Millburn: Mrs Heath: Gwen White: Hebden Knee: Francis White: Eddie Little: George Holton. (Wiltshire Times).

Memories of the Early War Years (1939 and 1940)

My MOTHER REMARRIED to Ralph Moore and moved from Bath to Westwood, taking me with her. We lived in a cottage in Upper Westwood; originally there were four cottages which had been made into two. We had a large garden, more than half of which was given over to vegetables. I remember Ralph growing cabbages, potatoes, peas, broad and runner beans, together with onions which he would lay out to dry in the spare room and then string together in plaits for the winter. He also had three rows of tulips which were a wonderful sight, and of course they would multiply each year.

When it was apple harvest time, he would go to the orchard and buy a tree. This meant he could have all of the apples from that tree and he would pick them and they would be laid out in the spare room through the winter. The smell of the apples remained throughout the house and I would often nip in during the night to pick one out and eat it. My mother would turn them regularly and any that were 'on the turn' would be used immediately for pies.

As there was no bathroom or toilet inside the cottage we would have to go to the bottom of the garden to use the bucket toilet. During the summer the bees would be buzzing furiously inside.

Also in the garden was a shed where Ralph did his odd jobs. This had a glass side where he could bring on his seeds. There was another shed near the back door in which he used to keep his bicycle and later, when he bought me an old bike, mine would be kept there also.

Running water was not available in the cottages and we would take a bucket to the standpipe at the end of the road to fill with water we needed. The water pressure was very low, probably because we were so high up, and we would have to wait a long time for the bucket to fill.

On wash day, generally Monday, my mother would use the rainwater from the water butt in the garden whenever possible, otherwise it was a long job getting it from the standpipe. The water butt was very large, at least ten feet high and contained all the water collected from the gutters on the roof of the cottage. She would have to light a small fire under the boiler to use for boiling the whites and used a tin bath for the other washing.

My mother felt very lucky, as Ralph had an electric kettle which he kept on a tray in the window. She cooked all the food on the old range and we had a coal fire in the living room - the front room was kept for best. Ralph's father also lived with us and I can remember him cooking his cheese on toast on the fire. He would hold a piece of cheese on a fork and let it melt down onto the toast.

During the air raids on Bristol, we would go to the Mushroom Quarry to shelter. We also had evacuees that stayed with us for a short time - a lady and her sister with a small son, but they were Londoners and returned as quickly as they could.

There were two buses, one day a week, from Bath to Westwood, early in the morning and then again late in the afternoon. This was a country bus which would take a very long time as it visited all the outlying villages. However, we could walk to Bradford and catch a bus to Bath from there and it would take less than half the time. Opposite the cottage was a small general store, selling anything and everything and the bus stop was just outside.

I was sent to church in Lower Westwood with Olive Sheppard who was a cousin of my stepfather, Ralph Moore. I remember the church was very small. Olive must have been fairly young, but a typical country girl with a broad accent. She spoke very loudly due to the fact that she looked after her two deaf parents.

There was an infants and junior school in Lower Westwood but no senior school. The senior school was in Trowbridge and Usher's Brewery would send out an old coach or charabanc to pick us all up daily.

Christine Evans (née Tye)

Avoncliff

Aerial view of Avoncliff

AVONCLIFF IS A HAMLET in the Parish of Westwood and comprises 27 homes (3 of which are actually in the parish of Winsley), several boat homes and a public house. The hamlet lies in the bottom of the valley formed by the River Avon and is divided into 3 sectors by the Kennet and Avon Canal, the railway and the River Avon. Avoncliff is dominated by the Avoncliff aqueduct, which carries the Kennet and Avon Canal over the River Avon and the railway and is bounded on its eastern edge by mill buildings and on its western edge by Ancliff Square, an imposing rectangular building formerly known as The Old Court.

The Residents
From its origins in the thirteenth century to the dawning of the twenty-first, Avoncliff has been home to many and varied residents. Weavers, millworkers, publicans, bargees, doctors, nurses, chaplains, gentlemen, workhouse inmates, wounded soldiers and hotel workers have all played their part in the history of the hamlet. At the turn of the millennium,

105

Avoncliff is home to an equally wide and varied group of people including computer specialists, professional engineers of many persuasions, teachers, a postal worker, a chef, retailers, construction managers, gardeners, a printer, environmental consultants, an advertising agent and a retired civil servant.

The Mills

There have been mills in Avoncliff from at least the sixteenth century, when a grist and fulling mill existed, under one roof, and since when it is known that a weir adjoined the mills. The mill on the Winsley side of the river had numerous owners through the centuries and in 1737 it was advertised for sale as a fulling mill. In 1880 it was used as a flock mill, and was used in the same trade until the Second World War, when it was owned by William Selwyn, who lived in Avonvilla. The present mill is dated 1883.

The mill on the Westwood side of the river was also originally a corn mill, and there are records of a mill standing on the site at the beginning of the eighteenth century. In 1763 it was converted into a fulling mill. In December 1791 an inquest was held on William Gibbence, aged 12, "who with many others, younger as well as older, was employed at Ancliffe Mill in Westwood in managing and working the late improved machines and engines for cloth making, and having inadvertently, in his playtime, buckled one part or end of a long strap of leather round his waist the other end was taken hold of by a large upright piece of timber, called the mainshaft, constantly going round, turning and working the engines, whereby he was whirled round with great force, his body bruised, his limbs shattered and beaten off, so that he was instantly dead". In the year 2000 the residents and owners of that part of the Mill, now known as Weavers Mill, state that, despite its name, the house has never, in fact, been used for weaving and that the ghost of William Gibbence does not trouble them.

The mill has had many owners over the years and, at one stage, appears to have been occupied by the miller, an agricultural labourer and three prostitutes. It was eventually bought by William Selwyn of Avonvilla, and residents of Avoncliff can remember both mills being used as flock mills. Flock was made from old clothes, stripped and washed - local children searched the pockets of the clothes for money and objects of interest. The two mills were connected by a length of wire above the weir to which a boat was attached to carry things from one mill to the other. In 1901, a disastrous fire resulted in the almost total destruction of the Mill, which was known then as the Avoncliff Rag and Flock Mills.

AVONCLIFF MILL,

In the Parish of Westwood,

1 Mile from the Town of Bradford-on-Avon, 3 miles from Trowbridge, and 6 from the City of Bath.

PARTICULARS & CONDITIONS OF SALE

Of the above-named

VALUABLE

FREEHOLD MILL

Situate on the Banks of the noble RIVER AVON.

With the extensive Water Power,

POWERFUL TURBINE WHEEL;

25 - Horse Power STEAM ENGINE;

CAPITAL MULTITUBULAR BOILER;

Together with the

Driving Shafts, Gears, and Wheels;

STEAM & WATER PIPES,

Throughout the Premises. Also,

About 3 Acres, 1 Rood, and 25 Perches of excellent

MEADOW LAND,

At present, and for many years past in the occupation of the Owner, MR. J. A. WHEELER, Flock and Waste Manufacturer, which will be

SOLD BY AUCTION

BY

MESSRS. FOLEY & SON,

AT THE

Swan Hotel, Bradford-on-Avon, on Tuesday, the 17th December, 1878,
At 3 for 4 o'Clock precisely, in One Lot.

For leave to View, and further particulars, apply to the AUCTIONEERS, the Mart, Manvers Street, Trowbridge, or to

MESSRS. MORTEN & CUTLER,

SOLICITORS,

Newgate Street, LONDON.

After the 1939-45 war, the mill on the Winsley side was first used to manufacture chlorophyll and, later, firelighters. It has stood empty for many years. The mill on the Westwood side was more fortunate - it became a tea garden, with boat-rides on the river. It is now an entirely private residence and still has the mill workings under the house. The millrace is regularly visited by Kingfishers and is home to a variety of aquatic life including Pike, Eels, and tiddly fish of all kinds.

The Cross Guns Public House, Avoncliff. (Paul Melling).

The Cross Guns
The central, twin-gabled, portion of 'The Cross Guns' is the oldest part of the building, though its exact age is not known. The Deeds, dated 1712, state that it was built 100 years earlier as an inn but the fireplace has been dated by several people at 1550. It was probably used by quarrymen, mill-workers and people using the ford across the river. Beer was brewed on the premises, and brewing 'holes' have been found in the stable floor. Earth and stones from the canal bed were piled against the back of the 'Cross Guns' during the construction of the canal, which necessitated the bricking-up of all ground floor windows at the back of the pub.

During the lifetime of the canal the bargees frequented the pub, often staying overnight, stabling their horses in the stable adjoining the pub and the stables behind the railway halt, which have recently been converted into a house. A landlord in Bradford found old records stating that a landlord of the 'Barge Inn' took "ladies of the town" to the 'Cross Guns' for the bargees' general amusement on Saturday nights. But the bargees did not rely entirely on the ladies for amusement - they bet each other to climb up the inside of the chimney when the fire was lit. Having reached the top they were prevented from returning down by their fellows who had stoked the fire!

One former landlord of the 'Cross Guns' also owned one of the mills and wages of mill-workers were partially paid in his own tokens, which had to be spent in the pub. In 1981, the landlord still had one of these tokens which, it is believed, dates from approximately 1805, when coins were in short supply. Millworkers Token Ale is still being sold in the 'Cross Guns' in the year 2000.

On 31 December 1999, the local residents of Avoncliff and the surrounding area gathered in the 'Cross Guns' to celebrate the new millennium. The festivities were organised by a small committee of residents and included the Pantomime 'Cinderella', produced and acted by residents, and a fireworks display launched from the tow-path on the north-western edge of the aqueduct.

The Old Court

The Old Court, a square horseshoe-shaped building facing north towards the river and situated at the western end of Avoncliff, was built as a group of weavers' cottages during the late 18th century. Over the years, 'The Old Court' has changed use from the Bradford Union Workhouse from 1836 to 1914, a convalescent home for the wounded soldiers during the 1914 - 1918 war, a residential hotel known as the 'Old Court' between 1922 and 1948 and a conversion to 14 self-contained flats from 1952 to 1987. It was eventually developed into 12 separate houses and changed its title to 'Ancliff Square' - the name it holds at the millennium.

Few records remain of its origins as a Weavers Residence: it was reputed to have been built around 1762 by a clothier, William Moggeridge, owner of the 'Dunkirk Woollen Mill' at Freshford, to house between 14 and 17 families (there is evidence of 17 doors) of handloom weavers. The men used the top of the building, which gave them the best and longest light, to weave broadcloth, while the women and children spun and carded the wool on the other two floors, which were also the living accommodation. When

The Quadrangle, Old Court Hotel, Avoncliff. (Dotesio).

completed the cloth was dyed and dried in a domed drying house, which still stands behind the main building.

With the introduction of machinery into the Weaving Industry, handlooms became redundant and the traditional hand-weaving woollen industry declined. In 1836, the building was bought and converted into the Bradford Union Workhouse, which subsequently housed 240 inmates. A chapel extension was added which also contained the dining halls and kitchens.

The 1851 census recorded that on 30 March there were 249 occupants of the Bradford Workhouse - 13 officers and 236 paupers. Twelve of the latter were identified as weavers or cloth-workers, including one Ezekiel Troyford, aged 81, probably one of many of the building's previous inhabitants unable to adjust to the Machine Age. Another cloth-maker, Theresa Love, aged 19, may have been responsible for the faintly discernible inscription 'LOVE' inside the beehive-shaped stone building used as a drying house for the woollen cloth. In workhouse days, it was used as a lock-up and mortuary. In a report by the Poor Law Inspectors dated 1864, the inspectors cited the following observations among many: "...Two wards are fitted up on each side of the house exclusively for infectious cases ..... The adult inmates are supplied with flock beds, the children with straw beds. Washing troughs are provided in all wards ..... The men are employed in garden work and breaking stones; the women in washing and needlework….. There is a paid nurse ….. assisted by pauper nurses ….. There is a chaplain ….."

The building ceased to be a workhouse in 1914 and, during the First World War was used briefly as a convalescent home for wounded soldiers. The wards were named after districts around Bradford, the people of each district being responsible for the social welfare of the men in the ward of its name. The wounded were brought to Avoncliff by rail, and daily a Red Cross boat ran along the Kennet and Avon Canal, into Bradford, taking convalescing men into the town. Mr Ted Powell, of Bradford-on-Avon, has told me how he and his sister ran from Bradford to Avoncliff with a horse and led the horse, pulling the boat back to Bradford, before they went to school. In Mr. Powell's words, "In summer it was fun, but in winter it was a terrible job!" One of the former patients recalled that patriotic inn keepers in Bradford would often provide the soldiers with free beer and, returning by barge along the canal, they were greeted by sympathetic nurses with stretchers to carry the 'legless' back to their wards.

Its conversion in 1922, when it became 'The Old Court Hotel', saw the chapel converted into a ballroom and restaurant and later, during the second World War, valuable artefacts from the British Museum were stored for safety in its basement. The Hotel had a fine porter's lodge, with a bell tower and a clock, which was sold for £16 when the lodge was demolished, and later resold at Sotheby's for £16,000. There was no need to go outside Avoncliff for entertainment - the hotel provided for all tastes; - tennis, croquet, table-tennis, and billiards, as well as having a fine dance floor. It was called "A gem in the Avon Valley".

The Old Court Hotel closed in 1948 and the building remained empty until 1952 when it was bought by the Dell family who started converting it into 14 flats to house themselves, their eight grown-up children and their families – their plans were abandoned before completion. Following two more brief changes of ownership, the property was acquired by Anthony & Prudence Dunsdon in 1971. They took up residence in 1972 with their 7 children (Isabel, Aidan, Julia, Alice, Thomas, Philip and Edmund) and spent the next 18 years, using mainly re-claimed materials, to improve the interior of the building. In 1987 they decided to return the flats into individual homes based on the original weavers cottages. They commissioned Bath architects, Tim Organ & Hans Klaentschi, to carry out the project which involved gutting the interior without altering the character of its Grade 2 Listed facade. Builders PRC took nearly 2 years to complete the development, depositing huge quantities of soil on the 2 acre plot (originally the workhouse gardens and site of the school for the children of its inmates).

Ancliff Down

It was on this piece of land, where the soil was deposited, that Anthony Dunsdon had the idea of using the redundant stone reservoir (which used to supply the workhouse with water) as a possible site for an underground house. He asked Hans Klaentschi, responsible for the Ancliff Square conversion to draw up plans for the project. An application to build it was submitted to the West Wiltshire District Council in November 1993. Although it received widespread local support, final planning approval was not given (following a public inquiry) until February 1995. Construction of the underground house by local builders, Shellard & Winter, began in April 1995 and was completed in August 1997. The Dunsdon family moved in at the beginning of September and began the process of landscaping the huge mound of soil left over from the excavation for the underground dwelling, now named 'Ancliff Down'. Many of the materials used in the re-making of the landscape were stones and pavings from the former workhouse school and from the old reservoir. Specifically, the stone steps up the banks (slabs from the floor of the reservoir), flagstones which had originally paved workhouse floors and the standing stones, dug up when the site was excavated. Also, timbers from the workhouse were used to make the treads of the staircase. In 1999, the Dunsdons erected a stone circle with a central stone and seven outer stones at 'Ancliff Down' to commemorate the millennium and their seven children.

Anthony Dunsdon served on the Westwood Parish Council for four years and was partly responsible for planting over 200 trees around the parish following the damage done by Dutch Elm disease.

The Kennet and Avon Canal

The Kennet and Avon Canal, which passes through Avoncliff is one of the most splendid lengths of artificial waterway in Britain and is a fitting memorial to the canal age as a whole. John Rennie (1761-1821) is famous, among other things, for building Waterloo Bridge, London Bridge (now transported and re-built stone by stone in the Arizona desert USA), Dublin Docks, the Bell Rock Lighthouse, the Lancaster Canal and the Kennet and Avon Canal. John Rennie was also famous for perfecting the use of ball bearings - he used them to reduce friction between moving parts on his

The Kennet and Avon Canal at Avoncliff. (R Bartlett).

canal swing bridges.

Work began on the Kennet and Avon Canal in 1790 (when Rennie was 29 years old) and it was completed in 1810. Rennie, who was both engineer and architect, received £350 for his efforts. The canal links the River Avon at Bath with the River Kennet at Reading and provides a navigable link between London and Bristol. The early residents of Avoncliff would have witnessed the canal being dug out of the Wiltshire countryside by the labourers nicknamed 'Navigators' (this is where the nickname 'Navvy' for building labourers comes from).

Work started on the canal at Bradford-on-Avon in October 1794. The Avoncliff aqueduct was originally planned to be placed above the Avon Mills but by an Act of 1796 its position was changed to its present site. Work commenced on the Avoncliff site in March 1796 and was completed in 1798. The aqueduct carries the canal over the River Avon and dominates the hamlet; unfortunately, its central arch sagged immediately after construction and John Rennie is said to have regretted using stone. The aqueduct consists of three arches and is 110 yards long. A stone at the top of the parapet in the bay on the railway halt side of the aqueduct bears the inscribed date of 1797. (There were vandals two hundred years ago!). The aqueduct has a central elliptical arch of 60ft span with two side arches each semicircular and 34ft across, all with V-jointed arch stones. The spandrel and wing walls are built in alternate courses of ashlar masonry, and rock-faced blocks. The cutwaters are continued up as graceful splay-sided buttresses, and across the top is drawn a Corinthian entablature, not a slavish copy of some Roman original, but a simplified version, Rennie's own design. The abutment walls have the attractive concave batter and are terminated by square buttresses and wing walls. The marks of the stonemasons who have worked on the aqueduct over more than 200 years can be clearly seen; the ancient alongside the modern.

The Aqueduct at Avoncliff. (R Bartlett).

The canal flourished until the coming of the railway - in fact it benefited for a time, when the railway was being built, for much of the material needed was carried on the canal. Unfortunately, traffic on the canal was never as heavy as the promoters had expected, and so the canal declined steadily through the 19th century. It also suffered from early railway competition as the Great Western Railway duplicated its route and undercut its tariffs. On 18 March 1851 the Company offered the canal to the GWR and the transfer of the canal was authorised by the GWR Act no. 1. which received the Royal

Assent on 30 June 1852, when the canal became the property of the GWR. Maintenance standards on the canal slipped and this, combined with a rapidly declining traffic, meant that, by the end of the1914 - 1918 war, navigation became difficult in places. As the railway prospered, so the canal declined and in October 1926 the GWR proposed to apply to the Minister of Transport to close it. Owing to pressure from County Councils, Parish Councils and landowners, the plan to close the canal was abandoned in April 1928.

Mr Ted Powell remembers the canal between the two world wars. His father, Mr Thomas Powell, had two beautifully decorated barges, each with two bunks and a stove, working on the canal. Mr Powell worked for his father, taking grain from Avonmouth to Devizes. Each sack contained 2 cwt of grain and, when loading the barges, men carried two sacks at once, there being no cranes. There were two men to each barge - one leading the horse and the other steering the barge. Quite often one horse pulled two barges, each with a load of 25 tons. There were two pleasure boats running between Bath and Bradford-on-Avon at this time, the 'Margarita' and the'Koronora'. Ted Powell also worked on these boats with a friend. The boats stopped for passengers at Avoncliff. 'Elbow Cottage', the house in the field beside the canal at Winsley Bridge, was a public house for bargees.

Commercial traffic gradually decreased until it ceased completely, but there was the occasional pleasure launch. The last regular traffic left the canal in the 1930s but still it remained open. By 1940 there were no traders operating on the canal and the chief income at the Bradford-on-Avon toll office was from the sale of permits to cyclists for use of the towpaths. One recorded source of income is - "Paid one shilling for carrying a corpse across the aqueduct at Avoncliff". However, great interest in the canal resulted in the formation of a Canal Association shortly after the 1939-1945 war to fight for restoration. Although many difficulties would be encountered, the canal was still navigable on 1 January 1948, when the Railway Executive took control. The last pre-restoration through-passage was made in 1951 by the narrowboat 'Queen' with the West Country artist, P Balance, on board. Numerous attempts were made to close the canal until, in 1954, a leak occurred between Winsley Bridge and Avoncliff aqueduct. British Railways were then concerned that the canal bank might give way, endangering lives of passengers travelling on the railway, which is below canal level, and the remaining water was drained from the canal. In December 1954 the Daily Telegraph reported the intention of the British Transport Commission (B.T.C.)

to abandon the canal. This proposal brought a storm of protest. A "Fighting Fund" was launched and a petition, carrying 20,000 signatures, was sent to the Queen. Despite all efforts, in April 1956, the B.T.C. was allowed to suspend its obligation to keep the canal open to navigation until 1960, when the suspension was extended to 1963.

In 1962 control of the canal was vested in the British Waterways Board and efforts to re-open the canal were revived; the Kennet and Avon Canal Trust was formed out of the Association and practical steps towards restoration were under way. Experiments began to find a way to re-open the canal from Limpley Stoke to Avoncliff. Re-puddling proved to be too slow and laborious and in August 1966 B.W.B. and the Trust looked for other methods. An experiment, using heavy gauge polythene, covered by concrete was abandoned in 1967 but in 1976 work commenced at Avoncliff using this method and the canal was lined as far as Limpley Stoke. The work was largely carried out by young men employed under "The Job Creation Scheme" and was completed in 1978. The aqueduct was lined with a concrete "cradle" and made watertight in 1980. Using volunteers to raise funds from all sources, and with steadily increasing inputs from British Waterways, the Trust catalysed the re-opening of the entire navigation as a through route from Reading to Bristol. This achievement was commemorated on 8 August 1990 with HM Queen Elizabeth II navigating through one of the locks at Caen Hill, Devizes (the lock now bears her name).

However, these restoration works were a beginning and not an end, and work has continued through the year 2000 to provide water supplies, repair leaks and maintain lock workings and bridges. Unfortunately, the aqueduct at Avoncliff was one of those structures requiring considerable repair work. It had been built with faulty stone which was obtained from the Canal company's own quarry midway between Limpley Stoke and Avoncliff and it has not stood the test of time well. However, with the aid of grants from English Heritage and the National Lottery, British Waterways commenced replacement of the faulty stone in 1998 and the work should be completed in the year 2000; it is gratifying to note that the craft of Stonemasonry is still alive in the year 2000.

The Boat People

Over the years that the canal has been in existence, its use has developed through the carriage of materials, the transportation of people on the 'packet boats' and, at the turn of the millennium, recreation and permanent residence. In the year 2000, the number of boat dwellers based at Avoncliff varied but approximately 10 boats, ranging from the large double narrowboat 'EMILY BRONTE' to the tiny fifteen foot 'URCHIN' have become a regular feature of the hamlet. The 'boat people' are part of Avoncliff's rich and varied culture and contribute a great deal to the community with some of the children attending the local school in Westwood.

The Railway

When the railway was constructed it consisted of a single broad gauge track, the width being 7ft-quarter-inch, though the cuttings, embankment and ballast were all built to take a double track of broad gauge. It was planned to open the 9-and-a-half-mile track from Bradford junction to Bathampton on 20th January 1857, but upon inspection by Col. Yolland, the permanent way was found to be very rough, and the opening was postponed. After further work this stretch of line was opened on 2 February 1857. Between 18-22 June 1872, the track was converted to the present gauge of 4ft 8ins, but was still a single track. Conversion to the present double track was completed on 17 May 1885.

The Kennet and Avon Canal was carried over the railway line by a timber trough on brick abutments. Isambard Kingdom Brunel, who was responsible for building the Great Western Railway, considered the section of track at Avoncliff one of the most difficult on the GWR, because of the hazard of burrowing under the canal.

There was originally no station at Avoncliff, though there were stations at Freshford and Limpley Stoke. A platform was constructed at Avoncliff in 1906. It must have been really busy because the quarry firm at Westwood had tracks running from the quarry, behind Avonvilla, across the aqueduct to a stone-yard between the canal and the railway line on the Bath (west) side of the aqueduct. Trucks carried stone to the stone-yard, where 60 men worked cutting stone; the stone was then transported by rail, from the railway sidings in the yard.

In the early hours of the 8 February 1998, a goods train was derailed at Avoncliff; fortunately there were no injuries. Rail workers worked continuously for 3 days to clear the line and to repair the damage to the tracks.

In the year 2000, the line through Avoncliff is part of the main South Wales to the South coast of England line and trains stop on request. At those times when the main line is under repair, the track is used by High-

Speed trains to London, via Westbury. Occasionally, the Orient Express passes through the hamlet and, even more rarely, steam trains. Both provide a contrast to the regular commuter trains and the high-speed Inter City Expresses.

The Tea Rooms

The 'Tea Rooms' situated on the south-western side of the aqueduct, have been providing refreshment to walkers and visitors since 1973. Originally, food and drinks were prepared in the kitchens of 'Avonvilla' and served on the lawns by Sybil Mumford. Later, the 'Tea Rooms' were moved into a converted stone building in the garden and were known as 'Teazels' for a number of years. Following a change of ownership at the turn of the millennium, the 'Tea Rooms' are now known as 'The Mad Hatter'.

The Art Studio

The Art Studio opened on 1 January 2000 in the small building between the 'Cross Guns' and 'Rennie House'. The building was previously used as a wash-house and, more recently as a bookshop.

Freda Ferne
Paul Melling
Robert Read

We are grateful to Beryl Prosser for her permission to include text and information from her book 'The Waistcoat Pocket History of Avoncliff.'

The Westwood Bath Stone Quarries

Upper Westwood sits above an extensive underground Bath stone quarry. For nearly two Centuries this quarry has played a significant role in the history of Westwood: still growing in area, the quarry is part of a living industry and an ancient tradition.

Underground quarries have been classified as mines since the Metalliferous Mines Act of 1872 and in subsequent Acts, it is a legal definition only. Here they are referred to as quarries, which is what they are and have always been known as.

Geological Beginnings

The story of the Westwood quarries began in the age of the dinosaurs, about 150 million years ago in the mid-Jurassic period. At that time, what later become southern England, was much further south at a similar latitude to the present day Bahamas and Florida. The Bath area, including the site of Westwood, was then covered by a warm, shallow sub-tropical sea.

The sea floor consisted of white limey sand, made of broken shells and minute round grains of precipitated lime called ooliths. In the Bath area these formed extensive underwater sand banks, which are now beds of Bath stone. Just south of Westwood the shallow shelf-like sea floor dropped off into deep water and today this sudden change marks the southern boundary of the limestone Cotswold hills.

Ooliths give Bath stone including Westwood Ground stone its texture and colour. They are round and typically no more than half a millimetre across. They comprise a central grain of sand or broken shell surrounded by layer upon layer of time (calcite), precipitated out from the sea water, rather than lime scale furring up a kettle in a hard-water area.

Almost half the volume of an oolith is space in the form of micropores, the much greater spaces between the ooliths are known as macropores. During burial of the sand banks by newer layers of sediment, natural calcite crystals grew and filled some of the micropores and most of the micropores thus consolidating the once soft sediment into hard rock. The large strong crystals binding the ooliths together is known to geologists as cement; it is the calcite cement which gives Bath stone all its strength.

The structure of the stone is the key to its ability to withstand the weather, particularly frost after rain. The more durable Bath stones are known as Ground stones, hence Westwood Ground stone is a good building stone if used properly. There are rules governing its use, in particular the stone should be laid on its natural bed, i.e. the same way up as it is found in the ground and it should be bonded with lime mortar, not hard grey cement.

Godwin's Quarry. Roadway in an area of circa 1850s workings, looking north. NB. The two very French-looking stone and wood props are a feature peculiar to this Quarry. (©D Pollard 2000)

Early History of the Quarries

Until the last quarter of the nineteenth century quarrying at Westwood was on a small scale when compared with the quarries at Box, Combe Down, and Bradford on Avon, all of which were producing Bath stone long before any quarries were recorded at Westwood. Medieval church builders seem to have ignored Westwood stone. Perhaps a later start combined with relatively poor access to the best markets for Bath stone, handicapped Westwood.

Despite the lack of detailed records, it is certain that the earliest quarry at Westwood was where the Bath stone strata or beds outcrop on the hillside high above Avoncliff. These hillside quarries eventually extended along the flank of the hill. They are still there, the footpath from Avoncliff Lane towards the working quarry runs through these old workings which are now the setting for modern houses.

In 1405 two quarries belonging to the manor of Westwood were let, one in Mandevilles Grove for 2 shillings and the other held by the Dogget family for 4 shillings. Both were disused by 1649. One of the two quarries working in that year was in woodland north west of Upper Westwood farmhouse. It was still worked in 1862, almost certainly by William Godwin of whom more anon.

In 1794 George Fletcher, the Inspector of Building and Works for the Kennet and Avon Canal, was looking for sources of building stone to build the canal. He wrote, "About stone, I have enquired and examined every place I could find, …. I have found Excellent stone for the Purpose within 150 yards of Avoncliff Aqueduct… which may be got down.. for 1/6 (7.5p) pr Ton by a small Machine and Railway".

In 1795 Thomas Green, a contractor, agreed with the canal company to build Avoncliff Aqueduct. Again he reported that he had found, "some excellent stone for the aqueduct contiguous to the work and has begun to dig the same". The contract was soon taken on by another contractor named James McIlquham.

In October 1796 the canal company agreed to pay John Hoddinott 14 Guineas (£14.70) a year rent for his quarry at Avoncliff, from Michaelmas (29 September) 1796 for one year and for as many years after as necessary. This is the old quarry bounded by Avoncliff Lane and the footpath up to Upper Westwood. In May 1797 a great portion of the west-end side gave way and killed John Cook who was working there. The canal company rented Hoddinott's Quarry until 25 March 1799 or later, (it was probably worked by James McIlquham) but the quarry has not been worked since.

At that time there was little geological knowledge; most canal contractors had no experience of working with oolitic limestone and local experience was often ignored in vain attempts to cut costs. The stone from Canal quarry was of variable quality as the condition of Avoncliff aqueduct showed before the recent repairs to the masonry.

William Godwin's masonry yard which was between Upper and Lower Westwood.

Godwin's Quarry loading bay in an area of 1840s workings. (© D Pollard 2000).

William Godwin

An estate at Upper Westwood auctioned in October 1809, included "two Freestone Quarries of the first quality, one of which is in full work". This was probably Godwin's Quarry, the first significant underground quarry in Westwood. The mouth of the quarry is near Avoncliff Lane, a date of 1804 is scratched on a pillar just inside.

The area of pre-1840 underground workings is very small and work may have stopped for several years. As the 1841 Census recorded no quarrymen living in Westwood parish, the 1851 census recorded three, including William Godwin, then aged 22, living with his widowed mother. Kelly's Directory described him as a quarrymaster as early as 1848 when he was aged only 19. It seems likely that his father had been a Westwood quarrymaster.

From small beginnings, William Godwin built up a sound quarry business over a period of 50 years. The eastern part of the extensive underground workings is due mainly to him. Events including vandalism, employment disputes, a murder and bad debts occasionally thrust him and the quarry into the news.

Most of the quarry output went down Avoncliff Lane to the canal. One Saturday in May 1861 a wagon laden with stone was standing in the lane when, "some evil-disposed person or persons, with intent to do serious injury to a horse, took two lynch pins from the two front wheels of the wagon". A Trowbridge Advertiser said, "Words cannot be found to denounce such dastardly conduct". Fortunately, discovered in time, no horse was hurt and no culprit found, despite a £5 reward.

Jesse Hobbs, a carter who left Godwin's service without giving 'just cause or lawful excuse' was summoned to Bradford Petty Sessions in June 1872 for breaking his contract of employment. Hobbs, who was paid regular wages of 12s 6d (62.5p) a week and given two pints of cider a day, was fined 10s (50p) and costs, or in default of 14 days' imprisonment!

The Godwin monopoly on Westwood stone was broken in 1877 when Randell, Saunders and Company Limited opened their new Westwood quarry. Their advertising claimed, "The Quarries have been worked in a primitive manner for upwards of a century". In 1880 Godwin countered with advertisements for stone supplied from the original Westwood Quarries, "established 150 years". Around this time he started a new quarry south of the original one. The new quarry was worked in the latest way with cranes and trolley roads, a horse engine or ginny ring pulled the trolleys up the slope shaft just east of the lane between Upper and Lower Westwood.

In the 1881 census William Godwin, then living at Lower Westwood, almost certainly at 'The Limes' (now known as 'The Old Malthouse'), is described as a 'Stone Quarry Master and Maltster employing 26 men', some of whom must have been involved in parish matters both as a Vestryman and Land Tax Assessor. A rise in status is indicated by January 1889 as he then described himself as a stone merchant when suing a Cambridge mason named Marsh in the County Court. Marsh owed him £4 15s 4d (£4.76), and was ordered to pay 6s (30p) per month. There were probably other similar hearings.

Sadly, James Cottle, one of Godwin's quarrymen, was fatally injured whilst at work on the surface in April 1891. A block set-up edgewise toppled over on him after being struck by another stone which the men were moving with a crane. He had worked at the quarry for forty years and lived at Staples Hill. This was the third and last quarry fatality at Westwood.

William Godwin died at the end of the century and his two sons continued to run the quarry business in partnership with each other. Both also farmed in a small way. The business began to decline, there was a severe recession in the building trade from 1904, and late in 1908 the older Godwin brother, Herbert William, who lived at 'Leigh Green Farm' became bankrupt.

The lease of the quarry was due to end in March 1907. The Godwins continued to work the quarry with less quarrymen for two years and it was then leased to Isaac Jones, a Bradford quarrymaster for 14 years from 29 September 1910. Jones died shortly after and the quarry was abandoned. By then, all the underground workings had joined up to form a combined area of 20,407 square meters (719,270 square feet).

Colin Godwin lived at 'The Limes', Lower Westwood, which was bought in 1908 by his wife Lydia. The property included stabling for 9 horses and an old two-floor Malt House with kiln and vat.

The Underground Mushroom Farm

In 17th century France it was discovered that mushrooms could be cultivated by seeding horse manure with the spawn of wild mushrooms. This led to a further discovery by a Monsieur Chambry in 1810, who found he could grow mushrooms in the underground quarries of Paris. Underground dampness, humidity and a constant temperature of 11°C, together with a suitably arranged air flow will create favourable conditions for mushroom cultivation.

Since 1914 most underground cultivation of mushrooms in Wiltshire has been by Agaric Limited and its successors. Between the wars, their forte was supplying large hotels and luxury liners such as the 'Queen Mary'. They were equally selective in where they got their manure - only the top racing stables would do.

They converted the southern part of Godwin's Quarry for growing around 1928. The few details known of their Westwood operation reveal a rather heroic but generally successful struggle. In 1934 production was halted because part of the quarry suffered severe structural damage, possibly caused by an earth tremor. The following year growing restarted in a smaller area. Then, in 1936, there was an outbreak of plaster, which is a competitive fungal disease.

The early war years brought problems, including a shortage of men (women were not employed on picking then), diesel engine fumes penetrated the workings and ruined crops. Then the ventilation fan failed for a long time. In 1949 excessive air entry made the quarry too cold for growing and heavy rain caused clay to flow in down the slope shaft. Growing ended around this time, although it still continues at Bradford. The square airshaft by the Bradford Road near Leigh Green was part of the ventilation system.

The Tump Quarry

By early 1875 Messrs Randell, Saunders & Company Limited, stone merchants of Corsham, had started work on opening a new underground quarry at Westwood. This quarry was known as 'the Tump' on account of a small mound near the mouth of the quarry. An important part of this new venture was a tramway to carry stone out of the quarry and down to the canal and to a new stone yard and railway siding at Avoncliff. In April 1875 they applied for permission to lay the tramway on the canal towpath over the aqueduct. The Great Western Railway, who had owned the canal since 1854, gave permission on 24 July 1877; by then the tramway had been made almost to the canal. The stone yard siding and six lever signal box was inspected by Colonel Yolland of the Board of Trade and sanctioned for use on 28 November 1877.

The tramway descended to Avoncliff by a double track incline. The loaded trolley was lowered by a cable which made a single loop around a horizontal sheave wheel at the crest of the incline and continued back down the other track to pull up the empty trolley. The sheave wheel was located overhead and the trolleys passed underneath.

This machinery was probably a bargain as it had been used in Cornwall for drawing water up an incline. It then had a lever brake, but when set up at Westwood a screw brake was fitted. For braking purposes the grip between the cable and the sheave wheel was provided by clips on the rim of the wheel which gripped the cable as it passed around the wheel. The clip drum, as it was known, was a successful arrangement on steam ploughing engines, but its application with a screw brake on the Westwood incline had disastrous consequences.

Left: The entrance to the Quarry in 1895. © Crown Copyright/MOD.

The incline was tested using loads of ballast averaging four tons in weight from July to late November 1877. On the morning of Saturday, 1 December it opened for normal traffic. The incline machinery was worked by the quarry foreman, Samuel Beaven. Several loaded trolleys had been lowered down and empties pulled up, when a trolley with a very big stone was brought out of the quarry to the incline head and attached to the cable. As the trolley passed over the top, Samuel Beaven screwed on the brake, but never got control of the trolley which hurled down the incline, thus propelling the empty trolley up the incline at great speed. At the top it somersaulted, inflicting fatal injuries on Beaven who later died at his Bradford home.

At the inquest it emerged that the clips on the sheave wheel had failed to grip the cable. The stone on the trolley measured 86 cubic feet (2.44 cubic metres) about 5.47 tonnes in weight. The jury returned a verdict of accidental death, mainly, it would appear, because the dutiful Beaven did not get out of the way of the trolley.

Below the incline the tramway ran down to the canal where there was a level section across the aqueduct followed by s steep descent into the stone yard. From the incline foot, the loaded trolleys ran down singly by gravity; speed was controlled by a brakeman who rode on the back end of the trolley. Early in January 1878 a brakeman got a severe shaking when he lost control and was thrown off his speeding trolley as it left the rails on one of the sharp curves near the canal. Empty trolleys were returned to the foot of the incline by horse.

In the late 1970s Cecil Mumford recalled two big stones in his garden being sawn into ashlar on the spot by his father, where they had been thrown by a runaway trolley.

The men working on the lower tramway and in the stone yard had the benefit of the nearby Cross Guns public house. The quarrymen's need for liquid refreshment was met in May 1879 when an outdoor licence to sell beer in Upper Westwood was granted to a Frank Sheppard at the Bradford Brewster Sessions.

Until 1939 most quarrymen were employed by their gangers who entered into one year contracts with the quarrymaster or firm to dig not less than a specified amount of block. They were paid at a certain rate per cubic foot. Usually the gangers did not employ the pickers who tended to freelance, although they certainly paid them for the square yards of picking done. This sub-contract piecework system led to disputes, mainly over pay; some disputes reached the courts. They are the best source for identifying who actually worked in the quarry; one example will suffice.

In November 1879 John Bond was bound over to keep the peace for six months, for cursing George Trueman for about twenty minutes and threatening to kill him. The next case revealed the cause of his anger: Trueman owed Bond £2 8s (£2.40) wages for 3.5 yards (2.93 square metres) of picking and 12 days work. He was unlucky - his summons was dismissed because the Master's and Servant's Act did not apply to the case.

A horrendous accident happened on 5 June 1880 to a young quarryman named Jacob Target. A block of stone fell over and crushed him. One leg was almost completely severed and he died 17 days later in the Bath United

Hospital. He had only been working at Westwood two days, having gone there from the Monkton Farleigh quarries. By this time, Jacob Beaven, brother of the ill-fated Samuel, was foreman at the Tump quarry. We know this because a quarryman named George Banks was fined a pound for giving him a black eye.

Randell, Saunders & Company Limited amalgamated with six other Bath stone quarrying firms in 1887 to form the Bath Stone Firms Limited. In January 1888 they offered a commission of 10% off the price of Westwood Ground stone delivered in barges at Avoncliff to James Cox of Bristol and Messrs Gerrish & Company Limited, provided they both entered into an agreement to buy all their Bath stone from the Bath Stone Firms. In October the firms reduced the price of Westwood Ground in Bristol by 1d per cubic foot, "and elsewhere when competing with Mr Godwin".

This may not have produced the desired result because in April 1889 they resolved to sell Westwood Stone until further notice at 9d (3.75p) instead of 11d (4.58p) per cubic foot in truck or boat at the following places:- Bristol and immediate neighbourhood, Bradford on Avon, Trowbridge, Holt, Devizes, Westbury, Frome, Warminster, Witham and Radstock. These places were to be "canvassed for Orders as early as practicable". On 25 November 1892 the Firms added Westwood Ground stone, delivered in railway trucks at Bath Westmoreland Road.

The Avoncliff tramway gave the Tump quarry efficient access to the canal and the railway, the latter giving access to a much wider market, whereas Godwin was totally dependent on horse drawn road wagons. This made little difference over the short distance down Avoncliff Lane to the canal but it confined most of his trade to the area of the Stone Firms price reductions.

The effect of price cutting on Godwin's trade in a growing market may have been small; however, it encouraged the Stone Firms to reduce their costs. Both William Godwin and the Bath Stone Firms leased their quarries. They paid a dead rent which was a guaranteed sum paid whether the quarry was worked or not, and a royalty. The royalty was a sum paid per square yard superficial, meaning every square yard of new ground quarried, which was measured at ceiling level. If the amount of royalty due exceeded the dead rent then the higher sum was paid.

The Stone Firms got a new lease from their landlord, Mr G B Marsh of Westwood in February 1890, extending the term and area granted in their existing lease. The new term was 42 years from 29 September 1889. The dead rent remained at £200 a year and the royalty was probably 1s/10d (9.17p) per square yard superficial. A wayleave was included to bring stone through from an adjoining area of new ground leased from Mr H W Tugwell of Crow Hall, Bath for 42 years from 29 September 1889 at £30 a year dead rent and 1s/10d (9.17p) royalty.

In August 1895 the Stone Firms persuaded Mr Marsh to reduce the dead rent from £200 to £100 a year during the term of the lease, to take effect from 29 September 1895. Marsh recouped some of it three years later when he advertised quarry land to let, and the Stone Firms quickly agreed to pay him £40 a year for about 30 acres of additional quarry land on the same terms as their existing lease, which is probably what he intended.

The price cutting war resumed after William Godwin died. In December 1900 they reduced the price of Westwood Ground stone to 11d (4.58p) per cubic foot in railway trucks at Avoncliff for delivery to Bristol and neighbourhood. The price was further reduced in May 1901 to 9d (3.75p) per cubic foot free on rail or free on barge for the Bristol district. Then in May 1903 the Stone Firms decided to stop quarrying Westwood Ground as soon as possible. The reason is not known but the timing coincided with the start of a long recession in the building trade. One man was employed outside until 1906 probably to load out stone from the stack.

Until 1914-1918 war was a period of great economy as sales of stone petered out and quarrying stopped in all the Stone Firms quarries. In July 1916 they sold the old sold stable and blacksmiths Shop at the mouth of the Tump, to a Mr Rickets; neither had been used for many years. Later they gave a year's notice to terminate their two Westwood leases from September 1917 with the object of getting the rents reduced. They got it down to £30.

Work continued in the Avoncliff stone yard after the war. Conditions were primitive; about 20 masons, apprentices and labourers were usually employed; there was no running water and the only power was a gas engine which drove a lathe and possibly a circular saw. Block stone was brought in from Box and Corsham in main line railway wagons, although some is said to have been brought down the tramway from Westwood around 1926. Some of the internal stonework for Buckfast Abbey was worked here. The yard closed in 1933 and the siding was removed in June 1937.

The Tump quarry was dormant after 1908, but the lease was renewed by the Bath and Portland Stone Firms Limited in 1931 for a term of 10 years. Digging started again in 1938, only to stop when war broke out in September 1939. The tramway is believed to have been lifted around this time but the

Above: Clearing the old quarry, 1942.

1945

THESE PHOTOGRAPHS ILLUSTRATE THE TRANS-
FORMATION OF THE ENTRANCE OF THE ANCIENT
BATH STONE QUARRY OF 1895 TO THE MODERN
UNDERGROUND FACTORY OF 1945. ONE OF THE

Left: The entrance to the Enfield Works, 1945· © Crown Copyright/ MOD

trackbed of the upper part of the incline can be seen in the woods. It passes over a former footpath by a, now, blocked up bridge made of recycled cast iron weighbridge(?) beams. The Firms renewed the lease for a further 21 years from 29 September 1941 and bought the freehold in June 1955. During the intervening years much of the quarry work totally transformed.

Driven Underground – 'The Treasure Cave'

Long before the war, the National Museums and art galleries took steps to safeguard their treasures and many were removed to safe locations. However, by 1941 an urgent need for more secure and secret accommodation led to the conversion of part of Westwood quarry into a museum store.

Work began in June 1941. Clearing and structural work was completed within six months. A struggle then ensued to lower the humidity from its natural level of over 90% to 60%. The store opened for use on 24 February 1942, but problems with the air conditioning plant continued into 1943.

Several museums shared the store: they included the British Museum, the Victoria & Albert Museum, the Imperial War Museum, Free French Museum of National Antiquities and the Bodleian Library also had a collection there. The treasures stored included the Elgin Marbles, the Crown Jewels, the Rubens Ceiling from Whitehall Banqueting Hall, the statue of Charles I from Whitehall and the bronze screen from the Henry VII Chapel in Westminster Abbey as well as many other less known but valuable artefacts.

After the war the various museums moved out, the V & A being the last to go in 1957. The store was maintained for many years afterwards.

Driven Underground – The Royal Enfield Factory

Bombing raids by the German Luftwaffe in the Autumn of 1940 had a devastating impact on British aircraft and weapons' factories; the Air Supply Board was ill prepared for such an onslaught and proposals were made to relocate much of the industry into protected underground factories. In June 1941 the Ministry of Supply invited the Royal Enfield Motor Cycle Company of Redditch to operate the proposed Westwood underground factory for the Directorate of Instrument Production.

Work started on clearing the workings in December 1941 and George Wimpey & Company were responsible for the building work of what became Enfield No. 2 factory. They employed over 200 Irish labourers on the conversion works which included sinking three new ventilation shafts and numerous boreholes to carry services and smoke flues for the small underground boiler-house. The factory was primarily laid out for the production of Predictors.

Output of No. 3 Predictors began in July 1942 and was followed by a range of other gun control equipment. Towards the end of the war, radar control equipment for the Bofors gun was developed. Late in 1946 a visitor noted, "intricate parts of guns, generators for testing aircraft and other component parts of secret devices used in war" were still being produced.

The wartime workforce was about 300, the staff and a nucleus of skilled workers transferred from Redditch, but three quarters of the workers were local girls and women, many of whom had no previous experience of factory methods apart from a short period of instruction at Government Training Centres. The welfare facilities included a special room where workers during the winter months received sun ray treatment twice a week. One wonders what the old quarrymen would have thought about that.

During the war when the air raid sirens sounded, the villagers of Upper Westwood were allowed to seek refuge in the main tunnel of the factory but were not admitted into the actual works. Queen Mary, who spent much of the war at Badminton, visited the factory on 30 March 1943. After the war restrictions eased, Trowbridge Chamber of Commerce chose the factory as the venue for their first post-war industrial tour in October 1946, when a happy gathering of members, wives, sons and daughters were shown around the factory, by which time only 200 workers were employed.

There was a long slow decline and despite production of the 700cc twin cylinder 'Constellation' motorcycle being concentrated at Westwood, the Royal Enfield underground factory closed in 1970. A small part continued in operation as an engineering works by Willet & Wilkins until 1987.

Quarrying and Storage Again

Bath Stone quarrying resumed at Box and Corsham after the war, but following the closure of Hartham Park and then Clift Quarry in the 1960's, the need was felt for a Ground stone quarry. Thus, attention turned to Westwood Ground stone. The Bath and Portland Group reopened part of the former Tump Quarry in 1974 and digging continues now by Hanson Bath and Portland Stone. At the time of writing in mid July 2000, the working headings are south of Godwin's Quarry under and around the lane between Upper and Lower Westwood.

A secondary use of the quarry also continues. Since 1987 Wansdyke

Security Limited have used a small area of the workings for secure data storage, including share registers of mining companies.

Digging the Stone

The Westwood underground quarry is unique; it is the only one where the continuity and abundance of archaeological evidence allows the entire progression from primitive underground workings to modern workings to be seen so easily. The archaeology shows that the basic method of digging stone at Westwood changed very little over the last two centuries, whereas the tools and equipment greatly changed, enabling a higher output of much larger blocks by fewer quarrymen.

Underground ceilings and the ground above is supported by pillars of unhewn stone, the width worked between them is known as a breach and the quarried space leading to the breach is a heading. The Bath stone stratum dug at Westwood normally comprises one very deep bed typically around 2.3 metres (7.5 feet) deep which feature dictated working methods.

The rock is traversed by natural vertical breaks known as joints which are normally spaced many metres apart which roughly follow a straight course and tend to run parallel with one another. Once a joint has been located in at least one heading, its course and location can be predicted in future digging. As the object is to get rectangular blocks, the aim, as far as possible, is to make the headings cross the joints at right angles. Quarrymen constantly read the ground; their pay and safety have always depended on it.

The practice at God-win's quarry was to pick out a very narrow slot known as a jad forward into the rock at ceiling height for a distance of around 0.6 to 1 metre (2-3 feet). An 'upright' jad was then picked at the side of the breach, from the front into the rock for the same distance as the ceiling jad. Then by picking out a vertical line of wedge holes parallel to the upright jad and offset about 0.6 metres (2 feet) to one side of it, the first block (known as the wrist stone) could be wedged and split off sideways towards the upright jad.

After removing the wrist, a quarryman could get into the wrist hole and pick an upright jad along the back of what would become the next block to be wedged off sideways towards the wrist hole. The procedure would be repeated across the breach to the other side of the heading. Quarrymen endeavoured to use natural joints to save picking either the sides of the heading or along the back of the blocks.

The 'frig bob' type saw was first used at Westwood in July 1840 for sawing

Godwin's Quarry. A pillar in early 19th century workings. The direction of working was away from the corner nearest camera. (© D Pollard 2000).

uprights or vertical cuts. Saws cut faster than picks, wasted less stone and yielded blocks that needed less scapling or waste to be chopped off. Blocks of stone that were sawn or free on four sides but otherwise still in situ were moved either by wedging off sideways using chips and wedges or shaken loose from the bed underneath by inserting a heavy iron bar under one side and jigging it up and down. Both methods continued to the end of hand working. Gangers and quarrymen bought their own tools, usually from the firm's blacksmith but also others and even ironmongers. Picks and scapling axes were re-steeled by the quarrysmith at the quarryman's expense.

Stones quarried at Godwin's Quarry in April 1849 were around 1.13 cubic metres (40 cubic feet) in size and thus weighed about 2.5 tonnes. A crab winch was used here for pulling and loading stone and it is still there today. Godwin introduced cranes later than everyone else. They doubled the size of block that could be handled and were used from the beginning at the Tump Quarry which was sending out blocks in excess of 2.27 cubic metres (80 cubic feet) by 1878.

Some wooden bedded cranes still exist, two in the western part of the Tump Quarry, including one made by Tilke & Smith of Melksham as part of a batch of six ordered in May 1899, a third one in Godwin's Quarry; a fourth one by the slope shaft bottom was recently taken down and buried in the tipping space.

Quarrying restarted at Westwood in 1974. Since then, cutting has been done with Mavor & Coulson Limited 'Samson' Arc Shearers – in essence, a tracked chain saw. Currently No. 6067 delivered by Moor Park Quarry at Corsham in 1948 is used and it is believed to be the only working example anywhere.

Above: Picking.
Matthew Blake setting up
a new picking cut with
Samson No. 6067.
(© D Pollard 2000).

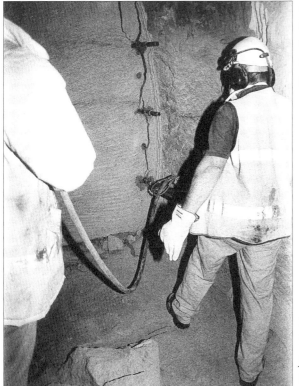

Left: Breaking out.
The block is breaking away
from the rock.
(© D Pollard 2000).

No. 6067 is fitted with a 2.3 metre (7.5 feet) long cutting jib; it starts the quarrying cycle by undercutting across the whole width of the breach (about six metres). Then the first third of the picking jad is done, followed by vertical cuts between the two; the Samson is repositioned in the middle of the breach to resume the picking, and then repositioned a third time to complete it. The remaining vertical cuts are then made.

The wrist is wedged off sideways using a breaker with a wedge shaped bit and a steel spacer block to pack the 114mm (4.5 inch) wide saw cut, then drawn out on the forks of the scoop tram, and laid on its side. At the present time the deep bed is actually two beds; a hole is drilled into the natural parting between them, a plug and feathers inserted, and a breaker used to drive it in thus splitting the stone into two separate blocks.

The other stones are broken out by drilling five equi-spaced holes down the back, inserting plugs and feathers (the modern equivalent of chips and wedge) in the top, middle and bottom holes, which are then driven in with the breaker. The block quickly cracks off through the holes and drops the 114mm (4.5 inches) to the floor, but stays upright. It is drawn out, laid on its side, drilled and split in the same way as the wrist stone; all the others are dealt with in the same way.

When the length of the scoop tram prevents it from being used to draw a stone out of a new side heading on its forks, a snatch block is anchored to the pillar opposite by means of a lewis inserted in it. A chain is passed around the stone, hooked onto a cable which is passed through the snatch block and hooked onto the scoop tram. This arrangement of ancient and modern technology allows the scoop tram to pull through an angle of 90°. When stone is pulled clear of the side heading it can be picked up on the forks.

Blocks are sounded for flaws, trimmed where necessary with a Hausherr air pick, cubed, (i.e. measured to find the volume), which is scribed and spray painted on the block, as is the block number and a vertical line to indicate the bedding plane to the customer. Blocks are stacked either underground, particularly in hard frosty weather or in the stacking ground outside. A small tractor tug and trailer shifts blocks out of the quarry, and loading outside is by forklift truck. Unsound block and waste is tipped in the old workings by the scoop tram.

Average output is 36 cubic metres a week. The current list price for Westwood Ground stone block is £227 per cubic metre if the volume is 0.59 cubic metres or less and £327 if the volume is 0.60 cubic metres or more, which it mainly is.

Despite modern machinery, digging stone underground still demands common sense, skill, team work and a lot of effort on the part of the three quarrymen who dig Westwood Ground stone. Matthew Blake, the Mine Supervisor, Chris Ramplin and Brian McKinlay. Work clothing now comprises a white helmet, green high visibility jackets, orange overalls and steel toecap boots; Peltor ear protectors and anti-vibration gloves are worn as are dust masks and goggles when needed. Essential personal equipment includes Oldham Crompton cap lamps and self rescuers to provide breathable air and prevent smoke inhalation in the event of fire.

The area being worked now is dry and conditions are good, while nearby there is a room for tea and lunch breaks. Working hours are normally 7.30 a.m. to 4.00 p.m. Monday to Thursday and 7.00 a.m. to 2.30 p.m. on Fridays.

For the record, Atlas Copco RH571 light rock drills are used; the breaker is an Atlas Copco machine; the air picks are Hausherr models, the scoop tram was made by Toro of Finland, and the air fan by the Bristol Fan Company. Other equipment used until recently included a Massey Ferguson shovel loader and two air motor cranes. Westwood was the last place where shears, (a medieval device for lifting blocks) were used for loading lorries until about 1997. There was an unsuccessful attempt in 1979 to use a Vamo rock cutter made by the French firm Aubertin & Perrot and in 1998 there was an unsuccessful trial of a wire sawing machine.

This is an abridged chapter from a forthcoming book, 'Digging Bath Stone', by David Pollard

BIBLIOGRAPHY

McCamley, N.J.:*Secret Underground Cities*, Leo Cooper, 1998
ISBN 0 85052 585 3
Palmer, Tim: *Know Your Stone, Bath Stone, Natural Stone Specialist*, May 1999
Pollard, David: 'Digging Bath Stone', *Subterranea Britannica Bulletin, Vol. 28* (1992) pp24-40,
ISSN 0307 1650
Victoria County History, Wiltshire, Vol. XI

SOURCES

PRO classes RAIL 842, POWE 7, IR 58
WSRO *Trowbridge Advertiser, Trowbridge Chronicle, Wiltshire News*
Census 1841, 1851, 1861, 1871, 1881, 1891

ACKNOWLEDGEMENTS

Thanks are due to many people for their help in making this brief account possible, especially to Matthew Blake, Chris Ramplin and Brian McKinlay, Keith Palmer, John Fisher, Trevor Poole, Colin Goble, the late Tom Brooks, Dennis Cole, and Peter Crompton of Hanson Bath & Portland Stone and its predecessors. The staffs of the Wiltshire & Swindon Record Office, Hampshire Record Office, Public Record Office and the Wiltshire Archaeological Society Library. To Nick McCamley for his unrivalled knowledge of wartime underground Wiltshire; Eric Durban of Wansdyke Security Limited; the late Ken Kettlety of Winsley and the late Jack Reade of Bradford who shared their memories of the Avoncliff stone yard with me; and the late Cecil Mumford of Winsley whose family once dug stone at Westwood and supplied horses to the quarry.

Where Did The Stone Go To?

The list of buildings built with Westwood stone should be a long one, but is in fact very short due to the lack of records. The stone was certainly used in Westwood itself; the church, however, is mostly of Bradford stone on a Box Ground plinth. William Godwin sent most of his output to Bristol by canal but only a handful of buildings can be linked to the Westwood quarries. These are listed below in chronological order:

1838	Holy Trinity Church, Trowbridge
1877	New Wesleyan Chapel, Cotham, Bristol – Dressings only
1886	New Baptist Schoolroom, Westwood
	Mr Godwin Supplied the stone at cost price
1889	Holy Trinity Church, Upper Tooting, London – Dressings only
1891	Hotel Victoria, Bath
	The Bath Stone Firms quoted for dressings, ashlar, rangework, undressed rangework and random block. The last two were to be delivered in boats at the quay opposite the site
1898	Empire Hotel, Bath
	The Bath Stone Firms quoted Major Davis 11.5d per foot cube for Westwood Ground delivered in barge at Bath, for the proposed Orange Grove Hotel
1975	Pump House Extension, Bath
1980	Halifax Building Society, Witney
1984	National Farmers Union Offices, Stradford-on-Avon
1985	Sovereign Court, Milton Keynes
1988	Mobil Court, London
1989	BBC Bristol Network Production Centre, Whiteladies Road
	Used with Portland and Monks Park stones
1990	Police Station Extension, Oxford
1990	Library, Bradford on Avon
1991	Library, Frome
1991	Barnards Inn, Fetter Lane, London
1997	Priory Hotel, Bath

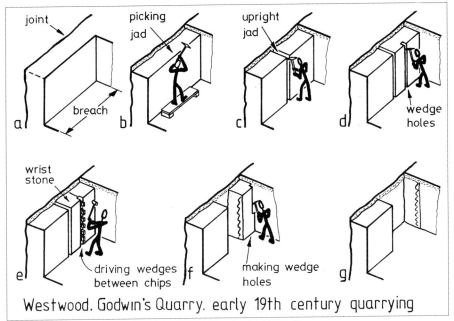

Diagram showing how stone was cut in the early 19th century

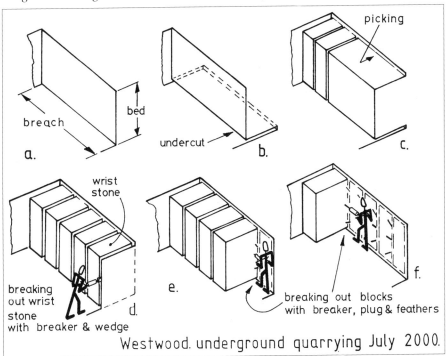

Diagram showing how stone is cut in the year 2000

139

Quarry or Mine?

In the *Westwood News* there was some correspondence about the differences of opinion on the naming of the hole in the ground which yields large lumps of stone. This letter was from Eric Truman:

Whether or not the correct definition of the workings near the Tump is Mine or Quarry is immaterial as far as I am concerned. The one and only thing I would say on the subject is that my memory goes back some sixty-five years and I can assure you that Pat Hobbs is quite right in her comments; pre-war everyone in the village termed it "The Quarry".

How well I remember, as small boys in the late 20's, how we would gather in the lane leading to the workings and peer through and over the hedge to watch with awe the huge cart horses sweating, straining and panting, pulling the huge blocks of stone along the rails. They were halted under the ancient hard winched crane standing in the centre of the open area before the main entrance where chains and ropes were attached to the blocks and winched on to the waiting wagons in readiness for hauling up the lane on to the road, again by huge horses.

I recall also the huge grindstone standing near the entrance upon which the labourers would sharpen the teeth of the massive saws used for cutting the stone under ground.

Reverting to the old crane, on leave from the army during the war I was invited down to the open space in front of the workings, probably breaking all the rules and regulations existing regarding the secrecy act in operation in wartime Britain. The very first thing I noticed was that the winch was no longer standing and had been replaced by an artillery piece - I think a 3.7" - not, I must add, as a weapon to be used in anger but merely, I believe, to be used as a test piece for instruments being manufactured in the "Shadow" factory.

Pat's remark concerning the use of the "Quarry" during the war as a National Air Raid Shelter reminds me now, more than fifty years later, of somewhat humorous happenings. Again, on furlough, I suppose some time in 1941, when the air raids on Bath and Bristol were at their heaviest, the sirens would screech out their wailing warning. I believe one of the flight paths of the enemy bombers was directed along the Avon valley. I am assured that, nightly, the second occupant of the 'shelter' was my dear old mother, complete with a cocoa-filled thermos, packet of sandwiches and a pinpoint torch. I stress the point 'second', as I understand the first arrival would invariably be one of the Air Raid Wardens. I don't believe my father even noticed his wife had left his side. I expect ours was not the only household in the village which had this experience.

I was born in the semi-gabled house on the top of the lane leading to the "Tump" and lived there for the first 14 years of my life. In the middle of one night when I was perhaps 7 or 8 we were awakened by a deep rumbling underground. Needless to say, no more rest was enjoyed upon this particular night. A first-light inspection showed a crack perhaps 3 or 4 inches wide stretching across our back garden and the lane itself. We were assured that there was nothing to worry about and it was merely a 'slip' near the entrance to the Quarry. During the day the crack was filled with rubble, dirt and clinkers etc., and to the best of my knowledge there has not been a recurrence of this happening.

'Dreadful Crime near Bradford-on-Avon: Double Murder'

So ran the headline in the *Wiltshire Times* of Saturday, 28 November 1885. A Westwood quarry worker called Jack Horton was the guilty party and it caused quite a stir. In a nutshell, he had "made a murderous attack upon his aged father, Edward Horton, of Westwood and then, leaving the poor old man in a dying state, walked to Tory, where he violently assaulted Charlotte Tarrant alias Lindsey, a woman of 44, with whom he recently cohabited. Horton died about noon on Saturday; Lindsey lingered until Monday evening when she expired".

Very few crimes receive such extensive coverage nowadays as did this one. The newspaper report is full of very flowery, not to say, lurid, details; "John Horton fanned his evil passions by strong drink, and with murderous thoughts in his heart he went home to seek for a weapon with which to wreak his vengeance on his grey-headed father and his whilom paramour".

He went to his father's house, suitably armed with an iron-headed implement with a 3-4 foot handle and proceeded to lay about the place until his father appeared at the top of the stairs asking what was afoot. "Helpless and defenceless though his father was, John Horton showed him no mercy. With his murderous weapon in his hand he sprang up the stairs, where stood this old man of 70, almost naked and crying for mercy."

There follows a detailed description of the wounds inflicted on the old man and how two neighbours, Samuel Hobbs and James Speedy, summoned by his grandson, came to assess the damage and then went to Bradford to fetch a doctor. "Meanwhile, Horton, with his hands reeking with blood but with his passion not yet appeased, went off to the house occupied by Charlotte Lindsey at Tory, a distance of a mile and a half. About 12.40 her neighbours were aroused by cries of "Murder!" and some of them heard sounds of someone running away while the cries were repeated. Help was speedily at hand and the unfortunate woman was found lying almost naked on the doorstep of the house, having been shockingly beaten about the head."

Apparently, John Horton reported for work at Westwood quarry early on the Saturday morning and a workmate, John Mead, asked him if it was true that he had beaten Charlotte Lindsey, to which Horton replied: "Yes, but the old man got it worse than she". John Mead then said that it was a thousand pities that Horton had had anything to do with it and prophesied that the police would soon come to arrest him. They left work at 1 o'clock by which time the police had not yet appeared and Mead said: "It will be a good job if they don't come but I expect you will have to go to prison over the job". Horton replied: "I don't know, when they hear both sides of the question. It may take £10 to get out of it, but there it's done, and I shall have to put up with it".

Horton was committed to the Assizes in Devizes and his trial took place in January 1886. The *Wiltshire Times* again reported it in full and gory detail, summing up thus: "The last dread sentence of the law will, provided there is no respite, and this seems hardly likely, be carried out at Devizes on a date to be fixed by the High Sheriff, probably on Monday, February lst. It is the invariable rule to allow three Sundays to elapse between a sentence of death and the execution".

The *Wiltshire Times* of 6 February reported: "The final scene of the terrible tragedy which sent a thrill of horror through the countryside on the 21st. November, took place on Monday (1st. February) at Her Majesty's gaol at Devizes, when John Horton suffered the last dread penalty of the law".

There then follows a full résumé of the trial and the events leading up to it before declaring: "At eight o'clock on Monday morning the sentence of death was carried out within the precincts of Her Majesty's gaol at Devizes. In place of the old-fashioned structure used at the last execution here, a new scaffold had been constructed in accordance with the Government regulations, on the south side of the prison, near the chapel. It is just outside the wall of the prison building, and within the outer wall, opposite the railway. A new doorway was formed at the end of a corridor, opening directly on to the 'drop'." Minute details of the structure and how it was assembled are given, followed by gruesome details of the actual death by hanging.

Finally, "since the conviction of Horton the cottage at Westwood has been renovated and there are now no signs of the terrible tragedy that was enacted there."

Ironically, the very next day, Tuesday 2nd Febraury 1886, there was a debate on Capital Punishment at a meeting of the Trowbridge Church Literary and Debating Society, on the motion that, "the object of Capital Punishment was to ensure the safety of the public, and that the abolition of such punishment would tend to the increase of crime." The motion in favour of Capital Punishment was carried with a large majority.

Susam Snailum

143

Some Interesting Buildings

The team which built Elms Cross House, later Granby House, showing Daniel Windo on the left, Albert Windo third from right and W P Hobbs, far right.

Granby House

In 1908, Isaac Jones, a quarry-master, commissioned the building of what was then called 'Elms Cross House' with the intention to sell when it was completed. But in 1913, whilst still incomplete, and soon after the death of Mr. Jones, the house was gutted by fire.

There was little doubt that the fire was the work of arsonists and blame was laid at the door of the Suffragette movement. Earlier that same week there had been angry heckling by women of the President of the Board of Agriculture, the Right Hon. Walter Runciman, when he addressed a farmers' meeting in Trowbridge. At the scene of the fire, carefully placed in a wheelbarrow standing conspicuously on the lawn, was a copy of "Suffragette" and, typed across the front of it the words: "For damages, apply Runciman of Trowbridge". The incident was reported at length in the local press, which obviously feared that this could be the start of a concerted campaign in the area. "We understand", noted the *Wiltshire Times*, "that special precautions are being taken to guard against further damage being done to property. More particularly does this apply to that connected with the family of a Cabinet Minister who has a residence not a hundred miles from Westwood and who is an avowed opponent of female enfranchisement. On Thursday morning there was picked up from the floor of the Trowbridge Picture Palace a scrap of soiled paper on which, in an apparently juvenile hand, was written: "VOTES FOR WOMEN" Keep your watchdogs awake. More of this to follow. "VOTES FOR WOMEN" D.W. While this was probably only a hoax, it was handed by the manager to the police who have it in their possession.

The House after the first big fire in 1913

"It should be noted that it appears to be extremely probable that the fire was not started in one place only and rapidly spread, but that every room was ignited simultaneously, for each part of the building was burnt out at the same time as the other; it must have been a simultaneous combustion in each room. One or two of the gables fell in, but in one that was left it was found that there was a crack from top to bottom, and the assumption is that this was caused by an explosion from the bottom or it might be from the heat of the fire.

Several bottles were discovered amongst the ruin and one of them had evidently contained oil. Too much importance must not, however, be attached to this circumstance for workmen have been engaged in the house recently. In the opinion of Mr George Earle, newly appointed Captain of the Fire Brigade, "a great quantity of inflammables must have been used for the conflagration to get the hold it did."

The house is described as "a modern house, standing in its own grounds about a mile from Bradford-on-Avon, and being built in the form of a square with false gables, this added much to its picturesqueness. The mansion comprised a spacious entrance hall, with a magnificent oak staircase, four large reception rooms, thirteen bed and dressing rooms, bathroom, kitchen, housekeeper's rooms and other offices. The contrast between the building on Tuesday and the remains on Wednesday can hardly be imagined; when our representative visited the spot the scene was one of desolation. Discussing the fire with a valuer that gentleman said he had never seen such complete havoc before. Not a scrap of timber (except for a few pieces of charred wood) could be seen anywhere. Only the four main walls remained standing with one or two inner partitions and a few gables which looked as if a strong wind would finally blow them over. Over £13,000 had been spent on the building and it was only ensured for about £5,000, the policy for this amount, it is interesting to note, being taken out a few days ago - certainly within the last month or so. Now the place is a pile of ruins."

No one was ever arrested or charged with the arson attack on 'Elms Cross House' and the mystery as to whether the "furnace" was indeed the work of the Suffragette movement was never satisfactorily solved. The newspaper report summed up: "Later enquiries disclose no new developments, and no arrests on Thursday had been made, the almost diabolical cunning with which the plot had been laid and carried into effect making the task of the police an extremely difficult one. A woman's footprint was discovered in the garden, but this is a very slender clue on which to proceed." Indeed.

In 1922, C.W. Darbishire, the last Liberal to sit as Member of Parliament for West Wilts, bought the ruins of 'Elms Cross House'. The Wiltshire Times reported. "From 1913 until the present, the bare walls have been a landmark of the countryside and it is Mr Darbishire's intention to have the house entirely restored as his permanent residence and that the work shall be completed as soon as possible. It is Mr Darbishire's wish that the work of restoration shall be entirely in the hands of local firms. The plans are being prepared by Mr. W.W. Snailum of Trowbridge and contracts for the building work will be invited only from West Wilts contractors.

"The news will be received with considerable pleasure in the neighbourhood, where Mr & Mrs Darbishire have achieved so much personal popularity. The work will be put in hand without delay and will provide very acceptable employment."

However, tragedy struck again when, within a few years of his purchase of the house, Mr Darbishire died of fever while visiting rubber plantations in Malaya; and his wife, it was reported, committed suicide shortly after.

Left: C W Darbishire, MP and his wife at Elms Cross House in the 1920s.

Below: The Granby Hotel after the fire in 1947.

From 1928 until the mid to late thirties the house was owned by people called Forster. They remember it as having 11 bedrooms, two tennis courts and 42 acres. Apparently, when the ground was being graded for laying the hard court, many Roman coins were discovered. There was also a croquet lawn, an orchard and paddocks, a cottage and stabling for 3 horses as well as garages for several cars. The annual Bradford-on-Avon fete was held in the grounds during that time.

The next chapter in the story of the house began in 1939 when a Mrs W Crossman, who had run the 'Granby Hotel' in Harrogate, had her property requisitioned for wartime government use. So she moved her business to 'Elms Cross House' and renamed it the 'Granby Hotel'. But in August 1947, the house was again gutted by fire! One villager who was a young lad at the time, remembers sitting on the five-bar gate behind the New Inn watching people running across the fields with bedding that they had "liberated" from the hotel.

Once more, the house was restored, since when it has been a private residence with the name 'Granby House'.

This article was based on information collected by Jim Johnson when he was the owner of 'Granby House'.

The Old Malthouse

In living memory the house called The Old Malthouse was, until it became a private dwelling, 'The Limes Farm'. Certainly, as recently as 1902, the buildings complex is shown as 'The Limes'. June Cooper, whose parents were at Hudd's Farm, then called Midway Farm, across the cross-roads towards Trowbridge, used to visit her grandparents there when they ran it as a farm in the 1930's, and it was still called The Limes when Mick and Peggy Rahilly moved in there in 1961. At that time the only farming done there was in what is now Limes Farm Cottage with the two fields north and east of the Old Malthouse garden. The Rahillys did not like the name 'The Limes' and, in conversation with a villager called Jack Battrick, he suggested they use the name 'The Old Malthouse' as that was what it had been.

The house dates from the seventeenth century but it was extended in the 19th century. In 1908 the house and fields (3 acres and 1 rood) were sold for £800. In the Inland Revenue valuation of 1910, the evidence of it having been a malthouse is found where it is stated: "The Old Malthouse with two floors, kiln and vat (now used as a store only), part at end converted to coachhouse". When one of the ceilings collapsed between 1988 and 1994, what was revealed was a floor with square holes in it and a lining of old matchboard with which it was customary to line the upper storey of a malthouse and a lot of barley grain and chaff was found up there. There was also evidence of special stalls in the barns outside, such as the type traditionally used in prize pig rearing. One of the barns bears the date 1693.

The New Inn

The New Inn was built around the middle of the 18th century. The large Tudor fireplace, which gives such distinction to the lounge, was apparently introduced from elsewhere. The cottages adjoining the pub were added some fifty years later, and forty years later still, the inn was further extended towards the road. If you stand outside the modern porch, which is now the entrance to the pub, you can see the original building very clearly. Take your life in your hands and cross the road and you can see the old door, which used to be the entrance to the pub years ago, when the pace of life was slower and there was less traffic. To the right of the door is a sash window, above that another window and above that, in the angle of the roof, a date-stone inscribed 1840.

Why was the New Inn so called? Because it was built on the site of the old inn or to differentiate between it and an older hostelry in the vicinity? No one knows, but there might have been an older hostelry. It is possible that a village the size of Westwood would have had an inn as early as the 15th century and it might well have been where the New Inn now stands. What it was called, if it existed, there is no way of telling. Sometime during the 1970's, the story circulated that the pub had once been attached to a Priory close by and called the Inn of our Lady. An inn sign at that time depicted a blue vase of flowers and the words, 'The Inn of Our Lady' but where it came from is a mystery. Ushers, the Brewery, have now been taken over, and records (if there are any) are not accessible at present, though I shall continue my enquiries. The McFaddens, who were Licensees during the later seventies, are sure it was there when they took over, and their predecessor, Jack Enderby, died early in the year 2000. Mrs Phelps, who was a Licensee for twelve years during the 50s and 60s says it was never called the Inn of Our Lady in her time, and in all my researches so far, I have not found a single individual who has any recollection of such a name being connected with the pub before the 70s.

Certainly, there never was a Priory and the Church in medieval times was dedicated not to St. Mary the Virgin, as it is now, but to All Saints, so whether there is any truth in the rumour at all seems doubtful. I should be very interested to hear from anyone who can shed any light on the matter.

Why the pub was built where and when it was is less of an enigma. In 1752, the road from Trowbridge through Westwood was turnpiked, the gate being on the south-east corner of the cross-roads at which the pub is situated. The new pub was undoubtedly built for the refreshment of those who had to pause on their way to pay the toll. The 'well-to-do', who travelled by coach and four (or more) had to pay a shilling; the less wealthy, who could afford only two horses, paid sixpence, and those whose carriage was drawn by one horse paid threepence. A lone horseman paid a penny. The cost to the farmer driving his cattle was tenpence a score. Sheep or pigs were half the price at only fivepence for twenty.

The first official written reference to the New Inn is in the Ale Housekeepers' Register, which covers the years 1822-1827. William Dyke, Victualler, was the Licensee, and William Fisher, Licensee of the Cross Guns at Avoncliff, was his surety.

William Dyke seems to have been a busy and prosperous man during the 1820s as, apart from running the New Inn, he rented some land, which no doubt he farmed, and is recorded as having been the tenant of no less than three properties on which land tax was payable. One of these was 82 Lower Westwood, the house immediately next to the pub, but it is impossible to discover where the others were. Why he should have wanted so much accommodation is another puzzle, but maybe he used it for his guests. Perhaps he was doing Bed and Breakfast? He was also obviously regarded as a reliable and trustworthy man as he was more than once during these years appointed joint assessor of property value for tax purposes and collector of monies. Interestingly though, like most of his village contemporaries, (the School was not established until 1841) he could not write, and documents are not signed by him, but bear his mark.

By 1831, however, William had given up his land and of the houses retained only eighty-two. Perhaps he had fallen on hard times, the population of the village having declined considerably for lack of employment.

There is no record to tell whether he was still Licensee of the New Inn. 1840 was the year of the expansion, but whether this was the initiative of William Dyke is uncertain. The 1841 census has William Dyke down as a

Publican, resident in Upper Westwood and also names John Mayell as a Publican living somewhere in Lower Westwood.

The 1843 Tithe map clearly tells us that William Dyke was still the tenant of Bartlett Little, owner of 82 Lower Westwood, which is surprisingly described as a 'house and beer shop'. Picture William serving beer in the front room, and his customers on fine days sitting on the bench outside. What was going on? The building which we know as the pub is said to be simply a house, tenanted by a lady called Grace Greenman and owned by George Clutterbuck Tugwell, whose family had been Lessees of the Manor Estate since the second half of the 18th century. He finally bought it outright in 1864. Did the pub perhaps close for business for some years while the alterations were being carried out?

William Dyke died in October 1843 aged 71. His burial is recorded in the Parish Register. There is no record of what happened after that until the publication of the 1848 Kelly's Directory, which names the aforementioned John Mayell as Licensee of the New Inn, so presumably by that time Grace Greenham had moved out and 82 was no longer functioning as a beer shop.

The next Directory of 1855 records that Henry Masters was the pub's Landlord. By 1861, he had been succeeded by John Stower, who continued until 1875, when Thomas Raines took over. Thomas and his wife, Maria, ran the pub for nearly twenty years and were followed in 1895 by Mrs Clara Holdway, who out-did them and remained in her post until around 1923 when Jasper Windo, known to all as 'Jesse' (possibly because he fathered seven daughters?) took over. Jesse beat all previous records and carried on until around 1950. Since then, Mr and Mrs Phelps, Alan Parfitt, Terence Ward, Jack Enderby, Frank & Sylvia McFadden, David Mitchell and Steve and Linda Thomas have all had a crack at the whip. The present Landlord and Landlady are Michael and Julia Matso, and long and happily may they reign.

At some time during the latter part of the 19th century, the ownership of the pub must have passed to the Rooke family, residents of Iford Manor, for in 1896 Ernest Wallace Rooke sold it back to H W Tugwell and G & T Spencer's Brewery in Bradford. Some time after that, Spencer's was taken over by Ushers of Trowbridge who remained the owners until the 1990s. The pub now belongs to the Wellington Pub Company Plc, based in London.

There must have been so many unrecorded changes over the years. It is difficult for us to imagine the pub as it once was. At some stage, someone thought it would be smart to conceal the ugly old stone fireplace and for a long time it was hidden and forgotten. Later in the 1970s, Frank and Sylvia McFadden stripped away the stud wall and were thrilled to find what lay beneath. At different times, we have such different ideas of what is beautiful. Twenty-five years ago, the visitor to the pub parked his car in a smaller car park, avoiding the crumbling pigsties, which occupied the top left-hand corner. He then entered the pub through what is now the inner door of the porch and turned either through a door on his left into the bar in which there was a pool-table and a dart board, or through a door on his right into the more salubrious lounge. If he had gone into the lounge, he might have found the room behind the fireplace; the 1840 room, curtained off, as this was used only at busy times. Alternatively, he could merely have stood still and rung the bell at the side of the hatch in front of him, in which case, in due course, some-one would have opened up and supplied him with cigarettes or a bottle or a jug of beer.

Since then, all these divisions have been done away with to create a much more open space and even what used to be a storage room has been opened up to accommodate extra dining-tables. The pub of the 21st century is not as in days of yore just a drinking house; it has to provide food, and people eating need more space. The porch has been added and a little terrace for those who like to watch the world go by. No doubt the pub will continue to change and be adapted to meet the requirements and tastes of the times. Just as it would be fascinating to step back in time to see what it was once like, so it would be equally wonderful to step forward to discover what the future holds. Only one thing seems certain and that is that the old New Inn will continue to provide sustenance and good company for many generations yet.

Jill Ross

With grateful thanks to the Wiltshire Records Library

One of the village characters used to have her favourite seat in the New Inn. One Christmas, the carol singers called in, as was their wont, and the Vicar was asking people to name their requests for their preferred carol. When the Vicar asked her, "And what is your choice?" he got the swift reply, "A dry cider, thank you Vicar."

Well House

In Upper Westwood the outstanding building is the 17th/18th century Well House. In 1911/12, when Mr. John Leslie, a retired diplomat and friend of Mr Ted Lister of Westwood Manor, bought it, it was called Greenhill House and consisted of the central building and a one-storey addition called the East Wing. The house, garden walls and gate piers are all Grade II Listed. For thirty-five years it was the home of Captain Christopher Marlow and his wife Nancy. Nancy writes:

"Mr Leslie did a tremendous amount of restoration work to Greenhill House after he purchased it. He built on the West Wing and raised up the East Wing from its one floor level to complete the visual symmetry. He put the house and grounds on the market in 1952 and the contents were also sold. I remember my doctor saying, 'Please don't have your baby on 24 November as I want to go to the auction of Greenhill House in Westwood!' This didn't mean a thing to us at the time and our younger son, Rupert, fortunately arrived on 20 November.

"A property developer, Mrs Bridget Senior (of Senior's Pastes) bought the house and then proceeded to divide it up into three parts and we had the middle portion. We moved in at the beginning of April 1953 with workmen still closing up walls and so on, ably assisted by our three year old, Roddy. We were followed shortly after by Dr and Mrs Fosbery, who bought the East Wing. This was a very happy arrangement, although they did suggest coming to have a look at us before finally buying! They were followed by Dr and Mrs Blair, who bought the West Wing. They also inherited the large back garden, with the exception of the top terrace where the well is situated. Originally known as the Well House and thought to have taken its name from Alvrie de Wella, who lived in the reign of Henry II, the original deeds stated that there was an obligation to supply the village with water in times of drought.

"We had the garden and one of the orchards opposite the house. A Mr Percy Tolman had the other orchard which bordered the side of the old cow-shed-cum-apple store. This he converted into a home in the 50's/60's and it became known as the Long House. There is a lovely garden behind the house with a long pond, now home to carp, and a double row of cypress trees which tapered away into what is now Chestnut Grove.

"There was very little traffic along the lane in those days - mostly cyclists and people walking to and from the Enfield complex. Sandy, our Dandie Dinmont terrier, used to sit in the middle of the road hoping for some excitement and he had several two-legged friends who would bring him 'tit-bits'. Bert Hazell, who had been gardener at the house and lived in the cottage now called Easthill, used to help us in the garden and Sandy would dig beside him for hours.

"All this seems a long time ago now and in 1987 we felt it was time to move. We were very fortunate to be able to build a new house in Great Orchard which enabled us to stay in Westwood where everything was so familiar and we had many old friends. It is also good to see the old Wellhouse so well cared for as well as regaining its original name."

Well House.

The Homestead (Westwood House)

First it was a little country cottage set in about 2 acres of land, owned by two elderly ladies with the name of Palin. The cottage was very old so, about 1898, they had it pulled down and had the Homestead and Gardener's Lodge built. After the Misses Palin moved on, the house was bought by Mr. Scott Seward, a director of Ushers Brewery, and what is now Orchard Close was the kitchen garden and pigeon loft area. Mr Seward was a keen pigeon fancier and racer. He lived there for many years and also had a liking for cricket and villagers tell of the time Mr Seward would pay sixpence (2p.) to those batsmen who could hit the ball into his garden from the pitch which was situated where Lister Grove is now standing. The village urchins got wise to this and then too greedy, dropping a ball over the garden wall and claiming the reward rather too often. The gardener was then put on duty during cricket matches to make sure the sixes were genuine.

The house was then sold to Mr Hebden Knee (Knee's of Trowbridge), who only lived there for a few years and the next occupant was a Mr Coleman of Bristol, but the writer has little knowledge of him.

The two Villa houses opposite the Homestead were built about 1913. It was intended that three would be built but the builder, a Mr. Isaac Jones, died before the second was completed. This was on land owned by Mr. John Marsh, who was the last farmer to live in Westwood Manor. Farm buildings were added to the first villa and it became known as Haygrove Farm, with the writer's father the first owner, who stayed there until he retired in 1950.

"Westwood Lad - 1921-1950"

The above article appeared in the Westwood News in November 1993.

When THE LAURELS was built there were the usual protests to the Council as the intention was to rase Westwood House to the ground in order to pack in as many new homes as possible. Original permission had been for three homes, but by April 1988 the number of dwellings had risen to fourteen. In the event, Westwood House was saved and the Laurels is now an established cul-de-sac.

*   *   *

In June 1977 the local paper reported that "plans for 32 houses at HAYGROVE FARM, WESTWOOD, were received with as little enthusiasm by West Wilts District Council Development Control Committee as they had been by villagers and the Parish Council. A previous application for the same land was refused in 1975 for the same reasons: the site is in a green belt, roads are inadequate and so is the sewerage. In addition, the village and the District Council are worried about extensive development at Westwood. Planning permissions already exist for another hundred homes which the Parish Council considers the maximum that the village can assimilate in the next few years.

When BOBBIN LANE was built, the contractors, Beazer, had hoped to build right up to the garden boundaries of Chestnut Grove but, when they were refused permission to extend their site that far, due to the quarry workings underneath, they generously donated that part of the land to the village in 1979 as a park for the use of the villagers with a covenant restricting any building thereon.

*   *   *

The properties in CHESTNUT GROVE have, as part of their Title Deeds, the following entry under "Charges Register":

1. The land numbered 1 on the filed plan is with other land subject to the payment to the Lords of the Manor of Westwood of a yearly rent of £25.5s.0d. variable according to the price of corn.

2. A Conveyance of land to the west of the land in this title dated 9 August 1962 ... contains the following provision:

The land tinted pink on the filed plan is with other land subject to the payment of:
(a) the yearly sum of £6 part of £10 charged thereon by Sir Edward Hungerford by Deed dated 19 February 1629 for the benefit of the poor of Hungerford in Berkshire;

(b) the yearly sum of 7/-d. payable to the Manor of Westwood

Education in Westwood

The very early beginnings of education in Westwood can only be guessed at but in an extract from an Education Enquiry, England and Wales, House of Commons, dated 24 May 1833 it is stated, "Westwood–Iford-Parish (Pop 390). One Sunday school (commenced 1821) is attended by about 8 males and 12 females, and supported by voluntary contributions."

In 1841 there was a School Sites Act. This Act encouraged members of the gentry to help provide local schools in rural areas. Following almost immediately on the heels of this act we find the first step towards a day school in Westwood.

There is a "Deed of Grant made the 25 November 1841 by the Dean and Chapter of the Cathedral Church of the Holy Trinity of Winchester in favour of the Rector and Churchwardens and Overseers of the Poor of the Parish of Westwood." 'The Deed of Conveyance of Land for the Site of a School' indicated that the said land contained, more or less, 11 perches (a solid measure of stone usually taken as 198 inches by 18 inches by 12 inches), and was to be under the management and control of the Rector of the Parish.***

The village school was then built in 1841 on the south side of the lane leading from Lower Westwood to Iford.

The Old School House extension under construction, 1892

157

We can be sure that at the time, the school was probably considered a great step forward in the life of Westwood. The population of the village was slowly expanding. The 1848 Post Office Directory states that the population of "Westwood cum Iford" is now 430 and there exists a National School for boys and girls.

One account tells us that in 1846 Westwood had two Sunday schools and the "day" school. There were 57 boys and 50 girls attending which seemed a very solid number of pupils when the general trend in attendance in Wiltshire schools in that year was stated as being 1 in 13 children. "A schoolmaster and mistress were paid £25 a year in salary and the total expense of £29 was met from voluntary subscriptions and payment of fees."*

One does suspect those numbers a bit because in another account I found that in 1859 the pupils taught by a mistress numbered 30 boys and girls, in the school affiliated with the National Society and supported mainly by subscriptions.**

There may have been a perfectly reasonable explanation for such a disparity in numbers because the attendance did seem to fluctuate greatly over the next few decades. This reflected a changing rural community and the creation of other day schools in outlying areas.

The 1867 Post Office Directory cites a further increase in villagers; now there are 469 inhabitants and the mistress of the National School is named as Mrs. Frederick Hobbs.

Once again school numbers seem suspect in relation to the total population because there is an account that on return day, in 1871, there are 13 boys and 12 girls attending the village school.**

Support of the schools in the area was still dependent on private donations and there is a lovely mention that a Miss Agnes Mary Bythesea made a bequest in 1875 for Sunday school prizes for children of Freshford and Westwood.*

There is no mention of the school in Kelly's Directory of 1880, but in the 1898 entry we learn that a School Board with five members had been formed on the 24th July 1882. At this time in Wiltshire there was a total of only 22 school boards in the county.

The Westwood with Iford School is now referred to as a Board School, "mixed"(boys and girls), with residence for 85 children, but the average attendance rate is cited at 75.

The school had been enlarged in 1892 to the building that we see today to provide for separate infants' classroom. There do not appear to be any records surviving from the school before 1899. In Jill Falconer's very extensive research paper for her teacher training, which has a wealth of information, she discovered that many of the old school logbooks were probably destroyed by accident and unfortunately many specific details are lost. However, there are some earlier recordings of the School Board Minutes and we can see that in 1895 there was a total of four teachers on the payroll. Mr. Charles Croft was the head teacher and in 1896 he received a salary of £5.16.8 per month, as this sum is recorded in the May 15th records as well as for the month of June. Emma Croft is also mentioned in the salary list but she receives only £1.12.6d.

The other two teachers were Florence Windo, receiving £4 and Edith Rose whose salary is stated as £3.10.0.

We can hazard an informed guess as to how the school was heated because there is a mention of Coke purchased for £0.10.0 and coal for £1. Various other sums are cited for cleaning closets, general cleaning and desks.

Certainly in the late 1890s we can see that regular attendance seemed to be an ongoing problem. Alfred Beavan, of Bradford-on-Avon, clerk to the school board, salary £10 per annum, was directed to write letters of caution to certain parents. The Education Act of 1870 empowered School Boards with the authority to make attendance compulsory and they tried to enforce the act.

Since Westwood and surrounding areas were primarily rural communities, a large number of the children's attendance was contingent upon the farming schedule. There is a complaint by the head teacher Mr. Croft that attendance dips in the potato-picking month of November and there are always truancies in the haymaking of July. Many times the children would have been kept at home to help out in times of need or perhaps sent elsewhere to work when funds were badly needed to help family finances. In the school board minutes of 1896, the schoolmaster reports that Maud Wilcox, underage and not having yet passed her "required standard" was working in a factory at Farleigh. Another mention, in Jill Falconer's report, tells of " Henry Moore age 10 driving cattle to market for one of the farmers". The need for regular attendance seems to have been an ongoing battle.

The weather also played a major part in the fluctuating attendance records. In 1899 there were 95 children registered at the school. Many of these children came from outlying farms and up the lanes from Staples Hill. Once the school at the Union Workhouse in Avoncliff was closed the children from there also had to make the trek to Westwood with Iford Church of

LOYALTY   HONOUR

Wiltshire County Council.

GENERAL EDUCATION COMMITTEE.

Attendance Certificate.

Westwood with Iford Council School.

This is to Certify that

Herbert Hobbs

was never absent from School, and never late during the Year ended 31st March, 1908.

W. Pullinger

INDUSTRY AND PROGRESS

England School. In inclement weather it would have been difficult for many of the children, coming by foot, to attend.

In 1908 the average attendance is 92 pupils and it remained steady until 1913 and then gradually decreased until 1930. The figures dwindled rapidly and in 1938 there were only 27 children who attended during that past year (Bd. Of Education, List 2, HMSO)

Very early on the average age of the students was from 3 to 14 years in contrast to today's 5-11 age span. However, in the late 1890's many students left at 9 or 10 years. The main curriculum most probably covered Holy Scriptures, Reading, Writing and Arithmetic. A move was started to make schools more uniform on a national level, hence the various name changes from National School to Board School to State School. There was also the trend to become non-denominational. However, in Westwood, as noted in an existing logbook from the school, "the vicar came regularly to examine the pupils in religious knowledge" and it is believed to be a practice that continued into the 1950's. Certainly the vicar was involved in the administrative decisions in conjunction with early school boards and headmasters.

Jill Falconer studied the old school logbooks very thoroughly in her paper and it is from her work that we gain a very good idea as to the curriculum of the children and the shape of their days. To quote her directly, " The Scheme, or curriculum, for 1899-1900 for Older Scholars was very rigid and included Repetition, Geography, Mapping, Drill, Singing and "Object Lessons". The scheme for the infants was much the same sort of thing on an easier level."

It seems that the structure of the school day was quite strict and allowed little in the way of diversity or outside excursions. It appears only after a favourable report in 1926 by HM School Inspector Mr. Purdie, where he described the pupils as "diligent and well-mannered, painstaking and accurate" that some changes seemed to begin. From Mrs. Falconer's report, and I quote, "In the same month the Headmaster proposed a course of cookery classes to be held for older girls at Bradford-on-Avon Secondary School. When these classes eventually took place during the following summer the headmaster comments, "This is the first time that any child from this school has been included in any special subjects scheme." Westwood seemed to be slowly emerging from its isolation."

It appears that changes were afoot and now teachers were sent on training courses, parents were invited in to see children at work on various projects, and talented students were being put forward to win "free" places for further secondary education in Bradford-on-Avon.

Over the years the atmosphere in the school changed with a succession of Headmasters and Headmistresses who each had their own personality and method of educating the children. As in Mrs. Falconer's paper, I too, feel that special mention should be made of one lady who dedicated her life to the teaching of the children of Westwood. Miss Edith Windo, born in the village in 1882, became a Pupil Teacher in 1897. She started as a teaching assistant under an apprenticeship system to the experienced headmaster. And from an entry in a school logbook, dated October 22, 1900 we learn that Miss Windo attended the Pupil Teacher Centre at Trowbridge. As years went by it is mentioned that she taught the older pupils and often stood in when the headmaster was absent. Mrs. Falconer states that although no formal mention is made in the logbooks of Miss Windo being "certified" she was known throughout the village as "The Teacher". Her career at the school spanned 47 years and eight head teachers.

Westwood School, 1936.

After years of falling attendance in the late 1930s another change came to Westwood with Iford Church of England School. The Second World War changed the face of Westwood with the expansion of the local population. Approximately 94 new homes were rapidly built to accommodate workers, many with school age children, in connection with the Enfield Works and the resulting war work for the Ministry of Defence.

It was soon apparent that the old village school was becoming inadequate to deal with the increasing number of pupils. Parents were beginning to complain of poor conditions in the mid-Victorian building that was beginning to show ever more serious signs of disrepair. The sanitary conditions for the children were far from acceptable and there wasn't a proper playing ground available. It must be remembered that by this time the school was 100 years old.

Only in 1954, and the subject of three deeds, was the question of proper sewerage for the school eventually formally addressed. In the first Deed of Grant and Licence, dated the 17 of December 1954 it is finally arranged, "to connect a main drain from Westwood with Iford School at Westwood, in the County of Wiltshire to a sewer belonging to the Minister of Works and to allow the Wiltshire County Council and Mr H J Sheppard to connect branch drains to the said main drain." ***

Many years followed on with vague promises of a new school and temporary repairs were made to try and rectify the worst of the problems.

Beryl Taylor, a secretary at the school, wrote an excellent article on the problems facing students, teachers and parents alike. Having firsthand experience she describes the terrible conditions which made the task of proper education nearly impossible.

Mrs. Taylor writes, " Despite repairs to improve inadequate facilities, the major problems of dampness, poor ventilation and overcrowding still prevailed. There was a total lack of hall space or area for physical education. The school also lacked adequate cloakroom and toilet facilities. Children's toilets were outside the main building; the cloakrooms were only 4ft wide, contained only two hand basins and did not have sinks or drinking facilities. There were no staff toilets at all on the site."

The younger children were taught in temporary buildings on what is now the site for the Westwood Social Club car park, an unlikely improvement from when they were housed in the Old Chapel, another Victorian building. As both these areas were across the road from the main school building this presented many extra difficulties.

Mrs. Taylor also tells us that the main school room had a partition and was also the "Head's study, medical room, store room and school office. This room also had to serve as an assembly hall, village meeting room and gymnasium so it could not be fully exploited as a classroom."

It is no wonder that the villagers began a determined campaign to rectify the problem of the school. In 1971 there was disappointment when the new school had not been included in the programme for 1973-1974. There was, however, hope on the horizon when a letter acknowledged that the land had been purchased. It was decided that Mrs. Thatcher should be contacted as she was the Minister of State for Education. Mrs Taylor, in her capacity as secretary to the PTA wrote the letter herself. More promises were made, and County Hall confirmed the new school was to be started in 1973-1974, then a date of April 1974. More disappointment was to follow when another letter was received and to quote Beryl Taylor's article again, " the Secretary of State regretted that since the school did not fall within the basic need category she was unable to give her approval at the present time."

In this article of March 1994 Mrs Taylor outlines the campaign and the persistence of the village and how eventually Westwood School was included in the 1974-1975 programme with new funds finally found and approved. The foundations were marked out on 19 May in 1975 and building of the new school was completed in April 1976.

The Old School House, closed in 1976 was now empty. In a memo for the Conveyance of Land for the Site of a School dated the 31st of May 1978 "the Charity Commissioners approved the sale of the site and premises of the former Westwood Church of England School by public auction."***

Permission was refused for the Old School to become a village hall or shop premises, but it was finally agreed and approved that it could be converted to a private dwelling. This building, now known as The Old School House, with others like it in the village, is a visual reminder of the past and the changing face of Westwood.

In 1978 the Westwood with Iford Primary School at the north end of Boswell Road, had an attendance of 120 pupils. The children of Westwood now had a healthy and up-to-date environment in which to enjoy the benefits of a modern education.

Kimberly Milne-Fowler

Sources

Jill Falconer's paper, written for her teacher training at Newton Park.

Winning the New School, by Beryl Taylor, March 1994
* *Wiltshire Schools: A Short History* by Arnold Platt (1956), (HM Inspector of Schools 1923-1953)
** *The Victoria History of Wiltshire Vol. XI*, published for the University of London Institute of Historical Research, Oxford University press 1980. (Section on Westwood by Janet H.

Stevenson)
*** All Deeds are Certified True Copies of Public Record Office Copies in possession of Mr. &
Mrs. Milne-Fowler

As a commitment to the future, the children of Westwood School have planted a
small copse of native trees along Farleigh Lane.

NORAH NORRIS came to Westwood School as a teacher in 1971 by which time the school was so well populated that there were mobile huts in the car park by the Social Club to take the overflow. In these huts Norah taught the infants. She and Mrs Harwood taught the 5-7 year olds in the same classroom, but they did not find that a problem. Norah's idea of teaching was quite unusual, in that she gave equal importance to the Three R's and what she termed "life skills". She remembers putting on a circus, arranging pretend weddings and learning about other countries, assisted by dressing up in the appropriate costumes. They also ran a restaurant and a bank, put on plays written about items Norah had heard on the radio and ran a school newspaper, for which the children would "interview" villagers using pretend microphones. Norah would tell Bible stories using her "finger puppets", which she was frequently invited to take to other venues. When the new school was opened, Norah found the open plan classrooms not at all to her liking and she retired shortly afterwards. When asked at her interview why she had only ever taught infants, Norah replied that she found them the most difficult to teach and therefore the most interesting. She occasionally sees her old pupils around the village but the majority have moved away.

Schooldays Remembered

I first went to Westwood school at the age of three in 1937 but had measles badly and the doctor thought I was too young for school. I restarted at five and so was there for the duration of the War. The school was divided into the Little Room for the under 7's and the Big Room divided in two by screens for the rest. My first head teacher was forced to leave because she had married someone of German origin, I believe. Everyone was very sad about that as she was very popular and a fine teacher. She was followed by Mrs Cowan who came from Northumberland. Each morning and afternoon began with marching into the Big Room to a tune played on the piano. Mrs. Cowan then said, "Good Morning Children" and we replied "Good Morning Mrs Cowan, Good Morning Miss Windo, Good Morning Mrs. Johns", bowing to each of them. This was followed by hymns and prayers. In the afternoon we sang "All good gifts around us....". When we were settled, if anyone visited we had to rise and greet them using their name if we knew it or "Sir" or "Madam" if we did not.

Our first teacher was Miss Windo, of whom we were in considerable awe.

She kept a ruler on her desk and was not averse to using it! She was not in the best of health and, at intervals, took medicine which caused her to screw up her face as she downed it. She taught us to read and write and useful things like tying up your shoelaces; for that we had special lacing cards.

In the morning break we were given a hot chocolate drink which was made in a huge brown jug with a plunger to mix and froth it all up; and in the afternoons we had to lie on the floor on oval grass mats for a rest.

Mrs Cowan did her best to eradicate our Wiltshire accents! When we reached the Big Room we had elocution lessons, each holding a mirror and reciting "I spy with my bright eye a boy on a bicycle riding by" and the like. She was excellent at teaching handicrafts. By the time we left the school the girls had each made a pinafore, a nightdress and a dress, every bit hand sewn and embellished with bias binding and tucking. We learned to make a shoulder bag from felt with embroidered flap and thonging to join the bits together. American cloth was cut into tray cloths and a design painted on with Japlac paint. We learned elementary weaving by stitching the warp through a piece of card and weaving with a needle. We made ourselves slippers and a beret this way. Our exercise books were covered with brown paper on which we painted our own designs. We learned to knit when we were in the Little Room and there was a green cupboard in the corner where the wool was kept. It was all one colour, a coffee brown, and it had been wound into balls in such a way that they looked like coconuts. We made ourselves pixie hoods from this brown wool decorated by a stripe of red around the front. I now wonder what the boys did while the girls were making all these things!

At that time the school buildings lacked any modern comforts. There were earth toilets, which were nobly looked after by "Uncle" Oliver Cooper, who lived opposite. The rooms were heated by "Tortoise" stoves which became red hot when well stoked. They were fenced in by an iron guard. In about 1942 a kitchen was built onto the Little Room so that dinners could be served. The food came from a Central kitchen. Before that there was no running water apart from the standpipe across the road.

In summer we often had our lessons out of doors. Our desks were moved outside and the girls donned attractive frilly bonnets made from blue, black and white check gingham. We even went further afield. I remember a play reading of "The Three Tassles" on the hump going down Iford Hill. We performed little plays and learned poems and had a firm grounding in the 3 Rs.

Each day we had exercises in the playground, standing in line. Many of the children already had plenty of exercise walking to school as they came from Midway, Avoncliff and Friary Woods beyond Iford.

When the war started, the windows were all protected with nets stuck to the glass and a cross of paper stuck to each pane. We all went to school with gas masks bumping on our backs.

Diana Polhill (née Moscoff)

I was about eight years old when I began at Westwood School and made friends with Sylvia Ockendon, Margaret Phelps and Diana Moscoff. I remember clearly the maypole with the different coloured ribbons; we all danced around singing and I thought this rather wonderful.

There was a boy in the class called Allan Farley. He was talking rather a lot and Mrs Cowan, our teacher, asked him to stop. He didn't, so she called him to the front and said: "Hold out your hand!" He did and, as she went to strike him, he pulled his hand away and she hit herself on the legs. Her legs were very red. She was furious and told him to turn around and she gave it to him on his bottom, with him grinning from ear to ear whilst he was being spanked. All of us wanted to laugh but we dare not, as Mrs Cowan was a very strict teacher. She was also a very good teacher.

My mother, Millie Housden, was also caretaker of the school and administrator of the school dinners. So embarrassing, as she used to pile up my plate and the plates of friends to overflowing, so generous was her nature.

I also remember a girl called Pamela Holton who used to say to me on the first of every single month: "Pinch, Punch, First of the Month" and I would go home all bruised. Mum told me to do the same to her, which I did. She cried and said: "I'm going to tell my mum of you." She never did it again!

Queen Mary came to Westwood in 1943 and I remember her distinctly as a very formidable lady. She was signing a guest book at the Manor and we children were clustered around. We were too scared to say even one word. I remember that none of us would do anything that would upset our parents or bring any kind of embarrassment to them. The wonderful thing about going to Westwood school was that it brought me the very thing that no money in the world can buy: Life-long friendship with Sylvia, Margaret and Diana. I emigrated to Canada when I was 20 years old and I am now 65 and we have kept in contact all that time.

Esther Farley (née Housden)

My father was a very artistic and inventive man and every year I would be dressed up for the Fancy Dress Parade at the village Fête. I can clearly remember wearing a bright red dress, a cossack style hat and carrying a large black cardboard bomb - it must have had some significance as I won first prize. Another time I was dressed as a baker, all in white with a chef's hat and carrying a loaf of bread on a tray suspended around my neck. I think that bread rationing had just started so again, my topical outfit won first prize! In later years my friend, Esther Housden, and I dressed up as "Gert and Daisy", the music hall stars. We wore our mothers' cross-over aprons and wrinkled stockings and carried a bag of shopping. Our potatoes kept falling off the basket and rolling over the road, which I'm sure must have delayed the procession.

I attended Westwood infants and junior school and clearly remember being interviewed in the summer of 1946 by Mr Rowntree, the Headmaster of Fitzmaurice Grammar School whilst sitting at a very old and decrepit desk in the junior school playground. No cushy classrooms in those days!

Esther and I were always pleased to see Mr Welch, the milkman. He delivered the milk by horse and cart, measuring the milk from a large churn with a ladle. And if we were very good he would give us a ride on the cart - I can still see the rear end of that horse bobbing along between the shafts and knowing exactly where his next stop would be.

My Mum was a member of the W.I. and was very proud to represent the Westwood Branch at their big annual meeting in London.

Looking back, I realise that we children had a freedom that youngsters today must envy. With my friends Esther Housden and Margaret Phelps, we would wander for miles over country lanes to Iford and Farleigh Castle, picking wild orchids and cowslips and every Spring I would collect primroses and violets to send to my Auntie in London.

Money was short but we all helped each other - no door was locked - and my Mum, known as "Ocky", always welcomed everyone. We didn't have the luxuries that are around today but I feel that our childhood in Westwood was all the happier for that.

Sylvia Billett (née Ockendon)

Fancy Dress Parade outside the Baptist Sunday School.

Village Shops

At one time there were many more shops in the village than there are today. In Upper Westwood there was an off-licence and general store at the house called Ashlers, first run by Amy Hazell whose husband had Upper Farm. She retired into one of the cottages at the top of the quarry and Evelyn Badder and her husband bought it. Mr. Badder was a builder and Evelyn ran the off-licence and shop. She did this for thirty years, keeping very long hours, from 8.00 a.m. to 10.00 p.m. until she retired in the mid-1970's.

Then there was the shop at the top corner of Lye Field Lane. After several years in private ownership and after a very unpleasant attack on the proprietors, it was bought by the Co-op who put in a manager. The manager did not live on the premises so Viv Dagger and his wife moved in late in 1967 to provide a measure of security. They only lived there for a couple of years until the Co-op sold the shop which then became the private residence it is today. He can remember that the building used to develop huge subsidence cracks through which you could put your hand and Mr Badder would come to fill them in. When it was sold, the people who bought it built a shell around the original building and created decent foundations.

Viv's introduction to the village was when he was working as a roundsman for the Co-op doing the Westwood bread round in 1959. Morris's stores in Freshford covered Mondays, Wednesdays and Fridays and the Co-op did Tuesdays, Thursdays and Saturdays. He remembers one family which used to have twelve loaves every Saturday.

Also in Upper Westwood, the Tump was home to two shops; one, run by Mrs Ada Horlock, sold sweets and groceries in the 1930's on the site of No.117. The other, on the site of Quarry Wood Cottage, was run by Mrs Ricketts and was a tea shop where you could take your own basin to have it filled with home made ice cream. Certainly, at the turn of the 20th. century, people used to come out from Trowbridge by pony and trap to take tea at the Tump in Westwood!

In Lower Westwood there was a bakery at April Cottage. The small building which was used as the bakery was in use as a garden shed in the

1970's and was then demolished to build a tall garage to house special horse-drawn carriages.

In the late 1960's Mr and Mrs Nurse built a store where there had been a row of cottages in Lower Westwood. The builders were Charlie Shepherd and his son Bert. Mr Nurse also wanted to build a garage/filling station on the same site but was refused planning permission. When the Nurses sold up, the shop was bought by Betty Towlson and her husband who moved in in January 1978. Mr Towlson died in 1981 and Betty continued to run the shop until October 1985 when she retired. The shop continued for a short while until the property was converted into flats and sold. That shop, too, was burgled, mostly for cigarettes and whisky in May 1984.

Westwood Post Office was originally at 37 Lower Westwood. In Kelly's Directory of 1920 the sub-postmaster at Lower Westwood is listed as Charles Windo. Mrs Laura Windo was the first Post-mistress and her daughter, May, helped her and took over when her mother died in 1949. The Post Office then moved from Number 37 to the old blacksmith's forge and was run by Mrs Gibson at the time when Mattie Barker bought it in 1963. In 1967 the new Post Office Stores was built in Tyning's Way and Mattie Barker moved to the new building and ran it until she retired in 1971.

BETTY TOWLSON, who ran the shop in Lower Westwood from 1978 to 1985, was quite a character, according to her daughter, Rowena Heard. Rowena and her sister could always tell if their mother did not like someone who came into the shop. She would puff out her chest and say, "Can I help you?" in such a way as to send a chill through any sensitive person. But she was very generous and always provided sherry and mince pies for her customers at Christmas. One local character regularly came in to buy a flagon of Dry Blackthorn cider and one day announced that it was her birthday. When she had left the shop, Betty made up a birthday hamper, containing not only another flagon of cider but a tin of salmon and other goodies to take round to her house. When she mentioned it to someone else in the village, she was told that the birthday was not for another six months - apparently, the customer enjoyed having rather frequent birthdays!

In very early 1982 Westwood was cut off for about 4 days in heavy snow. In order to stock the shop Betty had to ask the neighbouring farmer to help with his tractor. When the electricity failed, she wrapped the freezer cabinets in sleeping bags and newspaper and said to her daughters, "Let's shut. We'll boil some soup up, light the fire and put a note on the shop door to tell people we're here if they need us." But no sooner had this decision been taken than people started coming to the shop, so Rowena got out the old manual cash till, lit some candles and opened up again.

Above: Nurse's Stores, Lower Westwood Road.

Right: The Post Office in Lower Westwood Road dressed for the Coronation in 1953.

Below: Harry and Marian Thorne outside the Post Office in Tynings Way before handing over after five years to Francis Roberts in August 2000.

Present Businesses

Elms Cross Vineyard

The first person to plant vines at Elms Cross was Alan Shaw. He bought the fields and planted 2000 Muller Thurgau vines in the seventies. He had his first harvest in 1975, the year he had the house built.

Mr & Mrs. Roland Dunkley viewed the property in May 1987 and moved in just in time for that year's harvest. They bought an additional 5 acres and planted another five and a half thousand vines; a mixture of Reichensteiner, Pinot noir, Pinot green and a hybrid of Pinot blanc called Auxerrois. In a polytunnel they also planted Cabernet Sauvignon and Merlot vines. They updated the equipment and mechanised production in order to cut down on labour costs and had a tank capacity of 14,000 bottles a year.

The most they managed to produce was in 1995, a good year, and a bumper harvest yielded 8 thousand bottles. Thereafter the weather pattern started changing, yielding very poor harvests in '96, '97 and '98. The warm winters and the late April/May frosts meant production had sunk to only 1000 bottles. At that point they realised that it was no longer a viable proposition and decided that the last harvest would be in 1999 which, due to another late frost, yielded so poor a crop that it was not even worth picking.

Aged 75, Roland Dunkley decided to retire and tried to sell the vineyard as a going concern but, not surprisingly, with a negative income of £10,000 a year, there were no takers. So they sold all the equipment, and a digger came to root up all the vines into which they had poured so much hard work. The roots were burnt and now the land is leased to a local farmer for grazing. In just over 25 years a potentially thriving business had come and gone. However, the Dunkleys have since planted a natural tree screen, a small copse and are about to plant, in the autumn of 2000, truffle oaks. These are oak trees with the roots impregnated with truffle spores, imported from New Zealand. They hope to re-establish truffles in England with their first harvest due five years after planting.

English Table Wine
Bradford on Avon
Auxerrois
11% vol.
Estate grown and bottled at Elms Cross Vineyard
Bradford on Avon U.K.
75 cl.
Made from Auxerrois grapes grown at Elms Cross Vineyard

English Table Wine

ELMS CROSS

Bradford on Avon

Rosé

10% VOL e

ESTATE GROWN AND BOTTLED AT ELMS CROSS VINEYARD
BRADFORD-ON-AVON, WILTSHIRE, UNITED KINGDOM

75cl

Made from Pinot Noir grapes planted in 1990/1991 on a gentle south facing slope. The subsoil of broken limestone at Elms Cross is particularly suitable for the Pinot Noir grape.

ELMS CROSS

19   96

DRY

English Table Wine

ESTATE GROWN & BOTTLED AT
ELMS CROSS VINEYARD, BRADFORD ON AVON
10.5%Vol   WILTSHIRE, UNITED KINGDOM   75 cl e

Elms Cross Vineyard lies just outside the beautiful Georgian town of Bradford on Avon. The town has historic connections with viticulture being one of the forty-two vineyard sites mentioned in the Domesday Book.

This wine is a blend from the Muller Thurgau and Reichensteiner grapes grown at Elms Cross.

The vineyard, established in the mid-seventies, lies on a gentle South facing slope of six acres. The very favourable micro-climate and the sub-soil of broken limestone gives the wine it's special character.

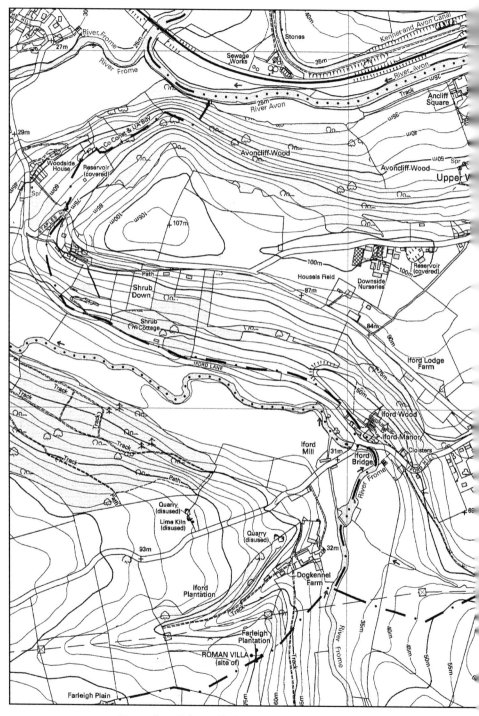

Reproduced from Ordnance Survey mapping on behalf of The Co

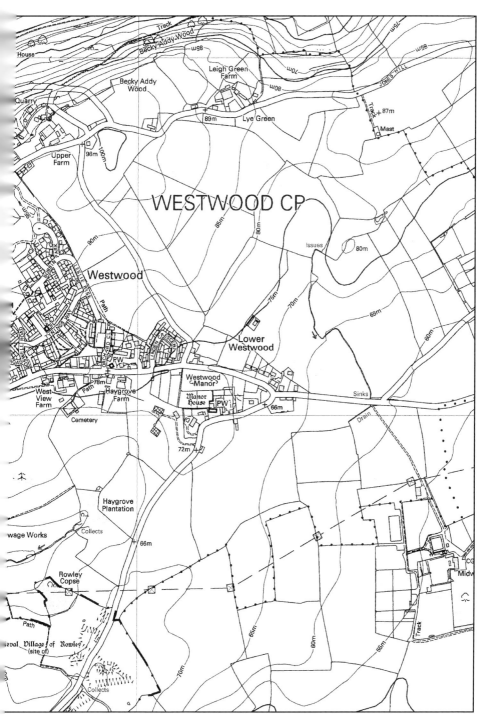

FARM SHOP

Entrance 200yds from the top of Jones Hill

Call in for:
Potatoes, Fruit, Vegetables, Eggs,
Hay and Straw

Open at weekends

J E MOORE & SONS
Tel: (01225) 865915

STAINED GLASS

Walter Ogilvie

113 Upper Westwood, Bradford-on-Avon
Wiltshire, BA15 2DN
Tel: 01225 862442

CREATIVE STAINED GLASS
Windows, Doors, Hanging Panels and Suncatchers
designed and installed

CAR SPRAYING   BODY WORK
USED CARS

INSURANCE   **John Shipp**   WELDING
WORK

111 UPPER WESTWOOD
BRADFORD-ON-AVON
WILTSHIRE BA15 8DN
Tel: (01225) 866626

149 ENGINEERS ROAD
WEST WILTS TRADING EST
WESTBURY BA13 4JW
Tel: WESTBURY 826506

S. M. SAY
CARPENTER & JOINER

Easthill
Upper Westwood
BRADFORD-ON-AVON
Wiltshire   BA15 2DF

(01225) 862151

R. SNOOK

BUILDER & DECORATOR

FREE ESTIMATES

TEL:
01225 863817

MOBILE:
0780 107125

8 LISTER GROVE
WESTWOOD
BRADFORD-ON-AVON
WILTS
BA15 2BR

Present and Past Activities

Westwood Art Club

As an offshoot of a defunct Bradford on Avon painting group, some enthusiastic local painters began meeting in the Westwood Parish Rooms in the early 1990's. From small beginnings the group has grown to fourteen members.

For the last two or three years the Art Club has mounted an exhibition of their work at the Westwood Flower Show; they also mount an exhibition on May Bank Holiday in the Parish Rooms.

Christopher Marlow

The Bradfordians at Westwood Manor

In 1992 the Bradfordians Dramatic Society was given permission by the National Trust to perform a play in the grounds of Westwood Manor. The play chosen was Shakespeare's "As You Like It", and so a tradition of mounting outdoor productions at the Manor came into being. The first night of the play "the heavens opened" and the action had to be transferred to the barn. This was very cramped but the actors managed superbly. The only problem was that the seats had become soaked whilst outside and red dye from them ended up on the audience. The following year the play was "Much Ado About Nothing" and this time the seating had a canvass awning and the audience were protected from the elements.

In 1994 it was felt that the Azis family should have a break from the disruption and "Twelfth Night" was staged at Iford Manor. Since 1995 a play has been performed at Westwood Manor every other year. The Society feels really 'at home' now and Westwood Manor is definitely their favourite outdoor venue.

Jo Tillion

Britain in Bloom

From 1983 to 1999 Westwood has been entered in the Annual National 'Britain in Bloom' competition. Entrants are in various classes such as Cities, Towns, Villages, etc., and the Judges are looking out for floral colour, reasonable evidence of planting and maintenance on the streets and pavements and reassurance that the work is communal rather than municipal.

For Westwood, this has meant that once a week on a weekday evening, a party of Residents has got together to plant roadside beds, tidy verges and hedges and install and maintain urns and hanging baskets. The profusion of springtime daffodils at the roadside throughout the Village is a reminder of the activities of the 'Britain in Bloom' crew.

Despite the chore of watering baskets and urns every day through summer droughts, the working party members derive great satisfaction from their efforts. The results have also been most satisfying to Westwood Residents. Working party members' area covers Upper Westwood, the Park, the Main Road, The Pastures, Boswell Road, Linden Crescent, the Church environs and the 'Westwood' road signs at the village entrances. The volunteers enjoy the camaraderie of outside work and have organised other social gatherings such as visits to other Contestant villages, house parties and fund-raising skittle evenings.

The Judges have usually awarded a certificate to the Village and on one glorious occasion, Westwood received a trophy! The initiative is supported by the Parish Council, which provides funds to purchase plants and hanging baskets.

David Lewis

Craft Group

In 1989 a member of the W.I mentioned that she would like to learn how to crochet and as a result of this chance remark the craft group was born, with a few ladies meeting weekly in the home of a member. The number grew until it was decided that the group should come under the umbrella of the W.I. and meet weekly in the Parish Room.

Over the years many crafts have been undertaken, including embroidery, lace making and tatting, macramé, rug making and cane and copper work (known as Repousse). Not all the crafts have been tackled by every member of the group (and in some cases only one or two have tried).

The craft group is always on the lookout for new crafts that the whole group can learn.

Hazel Scott

Darby and Joan Club (now known as the 60 + Club)

The Darby and Joan Club was founded in March 1959 with Evelyn Ledbury as the first Chairman. Meetings were held fortnightly in the 'Enfield Hostel' and the membership fee was 6d. per year with 3d. being charged each meeting for a cup of tea and a cake. Financial support came in the form of a cheque for 5 Guineas from Sir Michael Peto of Iford Manor and a grant of £5 from the Rural District Council.

A snippet from the January 1965 meeting - A member stated that she and several others had not been informed of the Carol Service. The Chairman replied that one of the members concerned had told her that although she was at the meeting when the Carol Service was announced, she had been engaged in conversation and had not heard the announcement. It was suggested that a bell should be provided to call members to order when announcements were being made.

In 1966 the 'Enfield Hostel' was demolished and the meetings were then held at the Social Club at a cost of 3/- per meeting.

In January 1970 Miss D F Lacey was elected Chairman and at her first meeting a unanimous vote lowered the minimum qualifying age of male members from 65 to 60 years. Following Miss Lacey's death, Lorna Bond became Chairman in 1971 and by 1977 there were nearly 50 members. In 1981 Pearl Rumbold was elected as Chairman and continued in the post until 1989, when Jo Cooper assumed the mantle until 1992. It was at this time that the club changed its name to the 60 + Club.

The current Chairman is Peggy Loader and the membership fee is £1.50p.a. and at each fortnightly meeting members pay 50p for the use of the Social Club premises and 30p for a cup of tea and a biscuit. Membership numbers are smaller now, but those who do attend enjoy the chance to get out and have a chat with friends and a game of Bingo.

Peggy Loader

The Choir at Westwood School

Bernard Newman took on the role of choirmaster in 1992. In his first year the choir learnt a short pop cantata "The Daniel Jazz" which was their contribution at a musical get-together of most of the primary schools in the area.

Over the years the Choir has given concerts at the school and occasionally outside. Their repertoire includes "Joseph and the Amazing Technicolour Dreamcoat". This year (2000) they were one of five small schools to take part in "Stonehenge" – a musical extravaganza based on the history of the famous stones.

Bernard Newman

Village Fête

In 1968 a Grand Fête was held on the old Enfield Sports Field (now the site of the new school), to raise funds for the newly formed Youth Club. A balloon race was organised and tickets were sold around the village prior to the Fete. The winning ticket was returned from France. The main attraction was the Westbury Model Steam Train Club, which gave rides to the public. A total of £60 profit was made.

Viv Hancock

Derek Bond opening the fete on 1 July 1950. He played Captain Oates in 'Scott of the Antarctic' with John Mills. (Wiltshire Times).

Westwood Flower Show

The W.I. Flower Show was inaugurated in 1987, at which produce, flowers, flower arranging, cookery and craft produced by Westwood residents were exhibited and judged. After the 1994 Show, the W.I. organiser, Hazel Scott, retired and responsibility for the Show went to a group of Westwood residents who became a sub-committee of the Parish Council. The Council, W.I. and Westwood News generously supported the 1995 Show after which the link with the Parish Council remained but the Show became self-supporting.

By 1999, the annual Show had become a major event in the Westwood calendar. Westwood wines, crafts, photographs and flowers were displayed in a large marquee erected in the field opposite the Church by kind permission of the National Trust Tenant Farmer, Philip Osborne. Vegetables were exhibited in the Nation Trust Barn of Westwood Manor by permission of the Tenant, Jonathan Azis, while a brass band played in the Manor

Grounds. Westwood's Art Club mounted an exhibition of their work in the Parish Rooms where the W.I. served teas and cakes.

The Show Committee attempt to offer a show in which all Westwood residents can participate. Although the standard is good, there is no attempt to outdo any of the major events such as the Frome Cheese Show! Interest is also generated by having, for example, classes such as 'the longest bean' and 'best compost'. Entries from Westwood School are arranged through the School teaching staff.

Prize certificates from the Westwood Show are sought after and there are also 5 silver trophies and ceramic 'Westwood Flower Show' mugs awarded to winners by a local celebrity at the Prize-giving.

The Show is a product of cooperation between Westwood W.I., Parish Council, Church, Tenants of the National Trust, Art Club, School and village activists; it relies on help from the Bradford on Avon Scouts, who provide tables and tents and the Bradfordians Dramatic Society, who lend their lighting. It attracts an attendance of over 500 visitors who come to see the 700 exhibits mounted by some 70 villagers. It is always held on August Bank Holiday Monday and is always a good day out!

David Lewis

WESTWOOD FLOWER & VEGETABLE SHOW

Bank Holiday Monday 28th August 2000

PHOTOGRAPHY

WINE   CRAFTS   COOKERY

CHILDREN'S SECTION

FLOWER ARRANGEMENT

Fruit, Flowers and Vegetables

Westwood Garden Competition

Every year, Westwood organises a competition to determine the 'best' garden. The objective is that any Westwood Resident may enter, so there are classes for best garden overall, best display of tubs, baskets, etc., and best front or back garden. An additional class separates those who have professional help in the garden from those who do it all themselves.

The competition is supported by the Parish Council, who donate cash prizes in the form of garden centre vouchers and there are also three trophies to be won, one of which is specifically for Senior Citizens.

186

Judging is carried out by an experienced Gardener invited from outside the Village and is undertaken in mid July. The entries range from large gardens worthy of inclusion in the "Yellow Book" to the modest front or back gardens of small dwellings. Prizes are awarded at the Flower Show prize-giving and the Competition is administered by the Flower Show Committee.

David Lewis

The Village Football Club

The Football club was formed in 1983. The club supports a junior section and through its history has brought many juniors through to senior level football. The junior section encourages the involvement of female players and while not able to attract sufficient numbers to form a full female side, acts as a feeder to the local town clubs. The Football Club has, for the last thirteen years, combined with the Village School Fete by organising a six-a-side tournament.

In 1984 the village had one team in the Senior League and by 1998 the Football Club had four Senior Teams, one Youth Team and one five-a-side indoor league team.

Over the years the football club has had several notable successes including Cup winners of the Bath Chronicle 'Charity Cup' in 1990 and 1994, League winners in 1994, runners-up in the Youth League Cup Final in 1989, runners-up in the 'County Cup' final and twice winners of the Sunday Independent `Team of the Day'.

The Football Club is seeking new changing facilities and hope to achieve this goal in the near future.

Sheila Biles for the Football Club

Mothers' Union

The Mothers' Union is an Anglican organization which promotes the well being of families worldwide.

Little is known of the early history of the first branch in Westwood. It was listed in the Diocesan Annual Report of January 1927 and the Cathedral Book of 1934.

The Parochial Church Council Minutes of February 1951 state that it was agreed to ask members of The Mothers' Union to serve teas on the occasion of the unveiling of the War Memorial.

There is, in church, a flower stand donated in 1958 in memory of

187

Olive Taylor (wife of the vicar).

By 1960 the branch had closed.

The original banner is now used by the present branch which was formed on 27 September 1976 under the leadership of Alison Guy (wife of the vicar).

Over the years, the branch has taken a full part in Mothers' Union activities with members serving at deanery and diocesan level.

A link was established with a branch at Wanama in Papua New Guinea. Letters are exchanged and a banner was made, dispatched and after several years, finally arrived at its destination in the remote little village of Wanama. Over the years we have been privileged to welcome to our homes in Westwood, fellow members from Australia, Kenya, Papua New Guinea, Sudan and Uganda, giving us a valuable and unique insight into day-to-day life in other countries.

All our work is grounded in prayer and three years ago we formed a special Prayer Group.

At present we have ten members,(two or three were at the meeting in 1976), who continue with outreach to the community and in support for a Women's Refuge, our Diocesan Family Holiday Scheme and our members worldwide.

Ann Hawke

Mothers' Union Members with Gloria and Mary from Papua New Guinea, 1988
Front row from left:
Pat Ashbourne:
Pat Hobbs: Ann Hawke:
Mary Padfield:
Back row from left:
Connie Christmas: Gloria and Mary:
Betty Hancock:
Dorothy Gwynn:
Beatrice Toogood:
Mrs Clark

Neighbourhood Watch

There has been an active Neighbourhood Watch in the village for the past 10 years and now there are twenty-five groups. The scheme, run in conjunction with the local Police, has been successful. It should be noted that Westwood does not have its own policeman, but relies on the community police system working out of Bradford on Avon.

Recorder Group

Recorders were taught in class time at Westwood School, but the new curriculum made it impossible to fit this activity into the timetable. For the past five years recorders have become an after-school activity and such is its popularity that there are three groups taught by two West Wiltshire Music staff and one parent – Debbie Newman. In 1997 four players - Anthea Osgathorpe, Lucy Johnston, Rebecca Newman and Matthew Pryor won an award at the Mid Somerset Festival.

Debbie Newman

Red Cross Club 1964-72. (Wiltshire Times) – see following page.

Red Cross Link

The first Red Cross link meeting was held in October 1966 at the Social Club, when 30 girls between the ages of five and twelve years attended. The girls were taught basic first aid, some home nursing, child care and basic hygiene. The group did well in competitions around the county. It wasn't all work; time was found for games during the weekly meeting and there were Christmas and Halloween parties. Outings were arranged to such places as Wookey Hole and Burnham on Sea, when brothers were also invited to come along. The Red Cross Link closed in 1973 due to lack of help.

Pat Hobbs

Safari Supper

The annual Safari Supper began in 1979, to raise money for the Church bells and was originally organised by Captain and Mrs Rahilly. The June event has been held every year since then and raises between £250 and £300 each year.

Betty Hancock

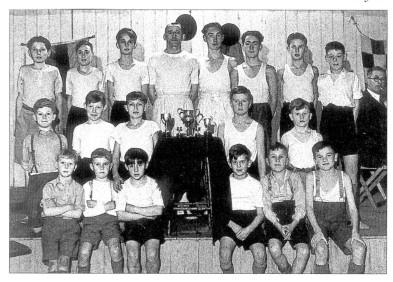

Westwood Boys' Physical Training and Gymnastics Class, 1947.
Back row from left: Charles Hudd; Alan Bailey; Alan Mercer; G H Holton (Instructor): Geoff Coombes; Graham Coombes; Peter Heath; Maurice Mumford; Middle Row from left: Michael England; Max Avey; Alan Farley; Edward Duggins; Norman Smith.
Front row from left: Mark Lamb; Paddy Harper; Stuart Hudd; Philip Heath; John Prosser; David Warner.

Westwood Skittles

Skittles as played in the village today can be traced back to the early 1920s when a Westwood team played in the 'Institute League' with their home alley at the Red Triangle Club, now the Westwood Social Club. During the war, two village teams, Westwood 'A' and Westwood 'B', played in the Bradford League with players cycling in for away matches. This continued until the Westwood League was formed in 1952/3, comprising teams from Peradins in Freshford and Westwood~ with matches played at the Westwood Club, the Greyhound in Freshford ~now a private residence) and, later, at the Barge Inn in Bradford. In the late 1950s a second home alley was started in the Enfield Hall. When this had to close, the new Enfield Club was built in 1966 at the upper end of what is now Bobbin Park~ but this was destroyed by fire in the early 1970s. Since then, all matches in the Westwood League have been played at the Social Club. The season which starts in October comprises 12 teams of six-a-side (six men's and six ladies'), and this is followed by a summer League with mixed sex teams.

Margaret Coombes

Westwood Social Club

In 1920 there was nowhere in the village for social gatherings. To remedy this, Mr Leslie agreed to provide some land and a number of villagers were driven by Mr Lister to Salisbury Plain to select a hut and settled on an old YMCA hut. This, when erected, became the village Social Club and was known for many years as the 'Red Triangle Club'. There was enough land around the club for cricket and football pitches and a tennis court. Cricket and football teams thrived in the village until the Second World War, when the land was requisitioned for building.

In the early years the club was well used, being home to the Carnival, Flower Show, Fur and Feather Show, Whist Drives and Village Dinners. The club was not licensed until after 1946 and as a result, three trustees were appointed and an elected committee established.

Early in the Second World War, troops were billeted in the club – it is believed on their return from Dunkirk. The Home Guard also used the hut as their base.

In the late 40's early 50's there was a lending library at the club. In the 50's and early 60's the club was thriving, with monthly cabaret and dances and skittle and snooker leagues.

In 1948 the club lands were gifted by Mr Leslie to the members of the

Francis White and Bert Hobbs building the new Social Club with blocks around the old wooden hut, which was then removed in the late 1950s

Francis and Gwen White behind the bar in the Social Club

Social Club under the care of the trustees and committee. The premises were rebuilt by Bert and Jeff Hobbs and Francis White in the late 1950's.

Pat Hobbs

In 1997 a new committee was formed and is now under the Chairmanship of Martin Fricker. Membership has increased by about 40% and the building has been greatly improved, including a refurbished bar, a newly painted hall and an extended stage. The exterior has been painted and new windows have been put in at the front of the building. A club member has made benches for the garden area.

Events which now take place in the Social Club include: Line Dancing, which is very popular, Bingo, winter and summer skittles, Snooker and Pool (on newly refurbished tables) and monthly special events.

The clubhouse is used by the 60 + Club and for engagement parties and wedding receptions. New Year's Eve 1999 was celebrated in great style, the club staying open all night and starting the New Millennium with breakfast the following morning.

Martin Fricker

Westwood Women's Institute

A meeting was held in the Century Hall (formerly the Baptist Chapel) on 19 September 1966. Four Voluntary County Organisers and thirty-one prospective members attended the meeting and a committee was elected. Mrs Valerie Newburn was the first elected president and Mrs Ann Truman was the first Secretary.

The W.I. is affiliated to the Wiltshire Federation of W.I's and is also a member of the National Federation, who organise days out, holidays abroad, courses at Denman College and day schools ranging from science days to crafts and cookery.

Through the years the W.I. has enjoyed many varied monthly meetings, outings when husbands and friends have been invited and at one time a small drama group was formed.

In September 2000 the Westwood W.I. are celebrating their 34th birthday. Three of the original committee; Betty Hancock, Sheila Pattrick and Pat Hobbs are still committee members and there are thirty-two members in the group.

Pat Hobbs

W.I. members in fancy dress, 1989
From the left: Leslie Chalmers; Elsie Blyth; Sheila Pattrick; Maureen Ledbury;
Betty Hancock (seated);Pearl Blyth; Hazel Scott; Monica Humphries;
Mary Padfield; Pat Hobbs

Westwood Youth Club

In 1967 a meeting was held in the School, with the leader of the Bradford on Avon Youth Centre. As a result, the village Youth Club was formed and first met in the school, but soon moved to the Parish Rooms at a rent of 5/- per week.

Badminton was played on Wednesday evenings between 7 & 10.30 p.m. and on Fridays snooker, table tennis, table skittles and various other games were played in the main hall. The small room held a coffee bar and record player and one cold water tap. This room is now the toilet, there being none at the time of the youth club.

The Youth Club closed in 1980, when the young people were invited to use the village club and they chose to forsake the Youth Club.

One of the greatest achievements of the club was when the girls won the Wiltshire Youth Clubs' netball tournament and proudly brought the cup back to Westwood.

Viv Hancock.

The Village Hall that never was

IT IS RECORDED that in May 1950 two ladies sought advice from the Education Department in Trowbridge regarding launching a scheme for a new village hall in Westwood.

In 1976 the Church of England Primary School had been closed and a Committee formed to consider purchasing this building to use as a village hall. Later this scheme was found not to be a viable proposition, primarily due to lack of parking space, and was therefore abandoned.

The idea of a hall for the village of Westwood had not gone away. In 1990 the Parish Council decided that a village hall was indeed needed. At a Parish Council meeting in 1991 a Steering Committee was formed to take the project forward. Later that year the Community Council for Wiltshire reported that "there have been several attempts to enquire about grants to help with the construction of a village hall".

In 1993 the Steering Committee became Westwood Village Hall Charitable Trust registered with the Charity Commission on 19 October. It was hoped to open the new hall in the Playing Field in October 1996.

The project moved on with outline planning permission, architect's drawings, public consultations etc., etc.. However, it wasn't to be and, to the immense disappointment of the Committee it became necessary, due to conflicting views and requirements, for the Trust to be wound up on 9 May 1997. It is now July 2000 - Fifty years on!

Mary Trevisick, Formerly Secretary to the Trust

WESTWOOD VILLAGE HALL PROJECT

GAINS MOMENTUM

The Village Hall Committee (Charitable Trust) was set up as a response to the Parish Council's initiative in identifying the need for a Village Hall for Westwood.

To date the committee is making positive progress with the project. Outline plans of the proposed site, together with Architect's drawings of the new building, and details of the facilities will be on show at a presentation to be held in the Parish Room on FRIDAY, 22 APRIL at 7.30 pm. All villagers are welcome to the presentation which will be part of the AGM, particularly those representing organisations that have an interest in using the hall. Members of the existing committee will be on hand during the presentation to answer queries and note suggestions from villagers.

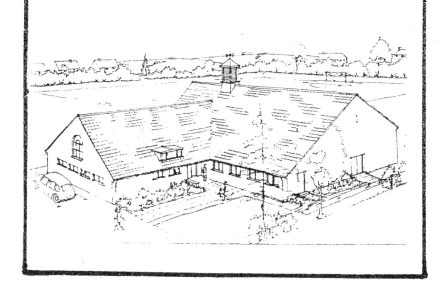

Architect's drawing of the Village Hall that Never Was by Bill Hind, RIBA.

Listed Buildings and Monuments in Westwood Parish

1. AVONCLIFF AQUEDUCT, partly in Winsley
2. CROSS GUNS INN, Avoncliff
3. BRADFORD UNION WORKHOUSE, 1-14 The Old Court, Avoncliff
4. CHAPEL, BRADFORD UNION WORKHOUSE, 1-14 The Old Court, Avoncliff
5. DRYING HOUSE, to rear of 1-14 The Old Court, Avoncliff
6. DETACHED COTTAGE, 109 Avoncliff
7. IFORD MANOR, partly in Freshford
8. THE CLOISTERS, Iford Manor Gardens
9. GAZEBO, Iford Manor Gardens
10. COLONNADE ON GREAT TERRACE, Iford Manor Gardens
11. WELLHEAD ON GREAT TERRACE, Iford Manor Gardens
12. GATE PIERS at WEST END OF GARDENS, Iford Manor
13. THE CASITA, Iford Manor Gardens
14. COLUMN, Iford Manor Gardens
15. SARCOPHAGUS ON GREAT TERRACE, Iford Manor Gardens
16. STEPS AND LOWER TERRACES, Iford Manor Gardens
17. WALLS AND GATEWAY TO KITCHEN GARDEN, Iford Manor
18. COTTAGE AT END OF ROW, 47 Lower Westwood
19. COTTAGE IN ROW, 48 Lower Westwood
20. COTTAGE END OF ROW, 49 Lower Westwood
21. TWO COTTAGES IN ROW, 78 & 79 Lower Westwood
22. THE NEW INN, Lower Westwood
23. FOUR COTTAGES (now three), 82, 83, 84 Lower Westwood
24. END OF ROW HOUSE, 86 Lower Westwood
25. THE OLD MALT HOUSE, Lower Westwood
26. WESTWOOD MANOR
27. BARN AT WESTWOOD MANOR
28. STABLE AT WESTWOOD MANOR
29. CHURCH OF ST. MARY THE VIRGIN, Lower Westwood
30. THREE CHEST TOMBS IN CHURCHYARD, St. Mary the Virgin
31. FIVE CHEST TOMBS IN CHURCHYARD, St. Mary the Virgin

31.   FIVE CHEST TOMBS IN CHURCHYARD, St. Mary the Virgin

32.   UPPER WESTWOOD FARMHOUSE

33.   TWO COTTAGES (now detached house), 26, 27 Upper Westwood

34.   GREENHILL HOUSE & WESTHILL (now called Well House), Upper Westwood

35.   GARDEN WALLS, GATE PIERS AND GATE, Greenhill House (now Well House)

36.   DETACHED HOUSE, ASHLERS, 130 Upper Westwood

All the above are Grade II Listed, with the exception of Westwood Manor and the Church of St. Mary the Virgin, which are both Grade I Listed.

Wells in Westwood

For a village situated 96 metres above sea level, Westwood is extraordinarily wet whenever there is a downpour! The ground is literally riddled with streams and springs and there are many wells to be found, particularly in Lower Westwood. Several houses contain their own wells, now safely under floorboards, and there are a few to be found in gardens. Orchard Close was built in part of the grounds of Westwood House and, in the boundary wall of Westwood House on the corner leading up to Orchard Close, there is a curved outline which is all that remains of a well which used to be there to serve the cottages that used to be behind that wall at one time.

There is still a well in the wall to the east of the New Inn which, when the village was expanding, was a source of great anxiety to some of the incoming parents. In one edition of the Evening Post in 1971, there appeared the following article:

"DEATH TRAP" WELL - ACTION TO KEEP CHILDREN AWAY

A door and lock will be fitted on a well near Bradford-on-Avon to keep children away. The well is beside a main road in Westwood and villagers say that it could be a death trap for children.

The well's gate has been broken and children can get in. The Parish Council asked Bradford and Melksham Rural Council to brick up the well. But the Rural Council has refused to do this because they say the well is sometimes used by builders mixing cement. Council Clerk, Mr Geoffrey Lamming, said that the door and lock would be fitted as soon as they knew the price. He stressed that the door would be the full height of the alcove and would be child proof.

This was the well which kept the cricket pitch watered in dry summers and, for the real villagers, to brick it up would have been unthinkable.

In Upper Westwood there is a well - a rather beautiful well - in the garden of the Well House.

Some Villagers Remember...

PAT HOBBS (née White) was born in Westwood and attended the village school. She was at the school at the time when the village absorbed the Enfield workers' children and the evacuees and it became very crowded. She then went to Fitzmaurice Grammar School in Bradford-on-Avon after taking the 11-plus but most Westwood children went to Clarendon School or Nelson Haden in Trowbridge. Most of the "incomers" went to Trowbridge schools as they were taken by bus because they, according to the "locals", were not used to walking or cycling.

In the early stages of the First World War, Pat's grandfather was posted missing and her Grandmother used to spend many hours at Avoncliff waiting for the narrow boats to come up the canal with the wounded who were on their way to The Courts, then a Red Cross hospital.

JEFF HOBBS was born in Upper Westwood and remembers walking to school in Lower Westwood through the fields. The fields used to take them through what is now Linden Crescent and the children were free to roam about and play in complete safety; they would be given jam sandwiches by their parents to take out into the fields where they would spend the day happily in total freedom. Having said that, though the lads from Upper Westwood would spend Sunday afternoons watching the building of the Enfield bungalows and hostels, the children from Lower Westwood did not like to stray to the Upper village alone after it had begun to be inhabited by 'navvies', Enfield workers and soldiers! Jeff's father was a stonemason who, after the War, was among those recruited to go to London and help with the repair of many of the bomb-damaged historic buildings.

DAVID WINDO was also born in Upper Westwood. His great grandfather and great uncle were in the team of builders who built Granby House (then called Elms Cross House) in 1908 for Isaac Jones (after whom Jones Hill is named).

Where Nos. 152 and 153 Upper Westwood are now, there used to be a

The Thatched Cottage in Upper Westwood which was pulled down in 1969.

pair of cottages called 'The Thatched Cottage'. They were so old that they pre-dated Deeds and belonged to the Diocese. When it came up for auction in the land sale of 1911, Mr Leslie of Well House bought it. David's grandfather had lived in half of it since the late 1800's and, before the cottage was knocked down in 1969, David bought what had been his grandfather's garden for £100 and built his own house, No 153A on it.

During World War II David used to take his sisters up to the field where the American soldiers were based when making collections for this or that good cause. Not having any English money, the Americans would give the children sweets, chocolate and chewing gum, which they found far more satisfactory! He was also enlisted to help in the paper collections in aid of the war effort. These were organised by John Knee, the son of Hebden Knee of Westwood House (after whom Hebden Road is named). The paper was collected in a cart which they trundled around the village.

David's great uncle Albert worked at the quarry and told of a Frenchman who came to work there. The Frenchman used to say that "if you 'ave a fat stonemason, send 'im to Asencliff". This was because the work was so hard and the conditions so hot that anyone working down there soon lost weight!

David also tells the story of a gardener at Iford Manor who was approached by Mr Peto and asked how he would be voting in the forthcoming general election. In those days staff were really expected to vote in the same vein as their employer. So the gardener replied that he would vote "same as you, Sir, same as you." "That's the ticket Harris - well done!" replied his employer who, as he walked away, did not hear Harris mutter, "I shall please meself Sir, same as you!"

VIC CHALLONER who lived at the corner of Iford Hill and Iford Fields, was a chimney sweep whose methods were unique. He used no ladders - just clambered up the roof and stuck the brush down the chimney, which inevitably resulted in an explosion of soot in the room downstairs. There were those who chose not to employ him and set fire to their own chimneys as a quicker and cleaner way to get the job done. He was also one of the gardeners at Iford Manor.

WESTWOOD NEWS was the monthly magazine produced for many years but, sadly, discontinued in the 1990's.

In the Christmas Issue of 1992, **Peggy Windo**, who died on 4 August 2000 at the age of 99, wrote of Christmas past:

"I came down from Scotland in the year 1911 at the age of ten to stay with my Auntie Edie and Uncle Hubert White, who at that time lived next to the Post Office in Lower Westwood, in a cottage in the garden of what is now Mr and Mrs Nurse's bungalow. I had come to visit my grandmother, Mrs Grace Hobbs, who incidentally was the great-grandmother of Betty Hancock, and stayed for one year. During this time I attended Westwood School.

At Christmas I stayed at the Post Office, which was in the front room of the cottage where Mr and Mrs Slade now live, to be with my Auntie Bella and Uncle Charles Windo and their three daughters, Dorothy, Molly and Gladys.

Christmas Eve was spent decorating the tree and making paper chains and cards then, after hanging our black woollen stockings over the brass bed rail we all four slept in the one bed. There was great excitement in the morning when we found an orange, an apple, some nuts, a few sweets and a sixpence wrapped in a bit of paper."

*In June 1977, the village **celebra**ted the Queen's Jubilee in style: Chestnut Grove had a street party, as did The Pastures; there was an Art and Craft Exhibition in the School Hall organised by the W.I.; in the evening an open air barbeque and dance was held outside the Social Club with roast pig, roast chicken and country dancing. Between 700 and 1000 people attended the various events*

Loyal Greetings from the village of Westwood, Wiltshire. June 18th 1977

St. Mary's Church, Westwood, 14th Century nave.

New Primary School, Westwood. Completed 1976.

Britannia Bridge, Iford, Near Westwood.

204

The Parish Council

In common with the rest of England and Wales the Parish Council was established in 1894, the inaugural meeting being held in the Village School at 7 p.m. on Tuesday the 4 of December when 41 people attended. The aim was to elect a Chairman and nine Councillors. There were 18 nominations all having been duly proposed and seconded on the appropriate form. This in itself was no mean feat as the election was only announced on the 20th of November; 427 votes were cast - a Parochial Elector was entitled to sign 9 Nomination papers so it is impossible to calculate the number of people who actually voted. Judging by the number of prospective candidates there was considerable interest in the event substantiated by the Chairman's opening remarks where he, "alluded to an alleged case of intimidation" - a Mr. Tanner gave a fully detailed account of the incident but this, alas, was not recorded. Furthermore, the Chairman reported that it was rumoured that Mr John Marsh had threatened to sack his men if they "went against his interest". Mr Marsh, it was reported, virtually admitted the threat but again his explanation was not recorded. From this rumbustious beginning the following nine individuals were elected:-

William Goodwin, Alfred Cottle, George Harris, Edwin Harris, Samuel Windo, Richard Harris, Frank Marchant, William Little and Thomas Hazell.

This initial interest in standing for the Council rapidly waned and the need to hold elections has been the exception rather than the rule. The original flush of enthusiasm was only matched in 1922 when there were seventeen nominations and in 1946, when there were eleven. By 1998 there were insufficient nominations to establish a quorum and for the first time in over one hundred years it looked as if village interests would have to be managed centrally by the District Council. Much was made of this sad state of affairs by both the Press and television and within a few days of the matter becoming common knowledge we had a Council!

The Council records present a complete picture of the social history of the Village and how it has developed over the past hundred years. It is interesting to note, and probably not surprising in a rural community such as Westwood, that the same problems recur. In 1915 it is recorded that "a long and desultory conversation ensued on repairing footpaths but no resolution was proposed". In 1920 the state of the footpath between Upper and Lower Westwood was such that the Council sanctioned sixpence in the pound on the rateable value of the Village to effect repairs. Footpaths have been the subject of many a debate over the years with the Council doing battle with landowners, horse riders, motor cyclists and the District Council. Indeed those who attended the July 2000 Council meeting will agree that the state of our footpaths is still a matter of passionate concern.

As far as basic amenities are concerned the Village water supply was augmented in 1923 but concern was still being expressed in 1929. The low pressure in the standpipes in Upper Westwood first raised in 1943 was still being pursued with the Rural District Council in 1947.

On August the 3rd 1933 at a special Parish Meeting it was decided by eight votes to two that the "Lighting and Watching Act" be adopted for the Parish. The Council had approached the local electricity company to provide the village with power and their local manager, who addressed the meeting, seemed very surprised that his employers had agreed, 'subject to income and expenditure matching', which could only be achieved by providing street lighting as part of the arrangement. The matter of lighting was still under discussion in 1949 when the Council agreed to provide one light at Staple's Hill and two in Avoncliff for the sum of £44.0.10 (forty-four pounds, no shillings and ten pence -old money); the installation of two lights in the park in 1998 cost £1588.00. School sanitation was of concern in the early fifties with the Council actively involved in trying to provide "flush loos" and the fight to provide a main sewerage continued into the sixties when it finally came to Staples Hill.

The Council try to meet Village needs and at the request of parishioners, have, over the years, provided a bus shelter, taken it down and all being well will replace it, at a different location during the year 2000. The dumping of cars, first reported in 1961, is still a matter of concern and occurred as late as 1999 when it was discussed with the Community Police officer. The provision of public transport, speed limits, school transport, street lighting (too bright, too much and not enough), have and will no doubt continue to feature on the agenda.

Bearing in mind the belief in some quarters, that the Council is responsible for every national and environmental calamity, it does its best to provide and maintain a pleasant environment in the village, to the annoyance, on occasion, of those whose planning applications it objects to and continues to do battle with the, 'Mummy and Daddy know best syndrome' prevalent in the District and County Planning Committees (in the past, for example after the last war, they forgot to tell the Parish Council that they had planned to build a few houses in the Village!). Members of the Council have laid paths and planted trees and now employ a Village Handyman to help keep the village tidy. Among its more unusual tasks are the management and maintenance of the Village Park and uniquely of the Village Cemetery and Churchyard. Kelly's Directory of 1919 states about Westwood, 'A cemetery of half an acre was formed in1883 at the cost of about £250 and is under the control of a burial board of seven members'. The Council also co-ordinates the production and distribution of the Village broad sheet.

The Council, over the years, has been asked to deal with many problems but did not consider the matter of the gentleman on a Sunday afternoon in 1957 who felled a beech tree (thus interfering with the Baptist Chapel service), fell within their remit. On the other hand, the problem of the Hungarian refugee football pitch running across a footpath was considered to be the responsibility of the Ministry of Works.

The current Council still continues to undertake the functions of its predecessors and, as will be seen from the above, the problems have not changed much over the last hundred years. There is a strong sense of continuity and one cannot help but wonder how the forbears of Bernard and Pat Hobbs would have viewed today's meetings - Samuel Hobbs was elected to the Council in 1896.

Terry Biles